OUR STORY: CANCER MOMS AND CHEMO BABIES

By Heather Choate and Stephanie Partridge

Dedication

In loving memory of our fellow KACM support group loved ones
who are no longer with us. We have fought together, side by side.
We have cried together, though hundreds of miles apart.
We smile and find hope in every miracle and good news announcement.
These are the cancer moms that gave life everything
and left their loved ones behind with memories to carry them through.

Adrienne Toth

Tara Boland

Jessica Fortney-Martellero

Meg Sager

Jennifer Doolabh

Crystal Hittle

Noelle Koosmann

Rachel Kerr

Courtney Jones

Beth Laitkep

Nok Sinart

Lauren Hubert Smoke

Amy Melton Warlick

Contents

OUR STORY: CANCER MOMS AND CHEMO BABIES

PREFACE

Life, in its simplest form, can be described as miraculous. Living this life in every moment with purpose and intention is an art that few possess. It is in moments of despair, pain, and anguish that we open our eyes to the masterpiece before us and within us that is life. Mothers with cancer face two divine milestones: life and death. The excitement and anticipation of holding the sweet, small baby; of feeling those first kicks on the belly; and of wanting the best for him or her, all while fighting a war within that begets destruction. Here, thirteen women find themselves facing this exact position. Labeled a miracle and a vision of hope and endurance of humanity, their stories have been shared in numerous social media articles and viral pictures; ten different news reports on NBC, ABC, CBS, and Fox News; the Today Show; local magazines and news stations; a national ad campaign by the American Cancer Society; People Magazine; the Wall Street Journal; an article in the New York Times; an LBBC brochure; blogs; "Fighting For Our Lives; A memoir," an Amazon Bestseller; local newspapers; radio; and a Yahoo feature article. Each of their voices is unique, and every chapter shares a glimpse into each woman's journey with cancer and motherhood. These are their stories, their fears, their hopes, their wisdom, and their unconventional friendship, and I am proud and honored to be among them. – *Stephanie Partridge*

CHAPTER ONE: DIANA

- Diagnosed 5 August 2015 *(23 weeks pregnant)*
- Stage 3A ER and PR positive HER negative invasive ductal carcinoma, grade 3
- Lumpectomy and node biopsy at 25 weeks
- Three rounds Adriamycin/Cytoxan while pregnant
- Delivered 20 November 2015
- One more round of AC, 12 rounds of Taxol, double mastectomy with DIEP reconstruction, 25 days radiation, and ovary removal after delivery.

I don't think I have ever accepted the possibility I could die. I know, logically, breast cancer could kill me, but deep down I don't really believe it will happen to me. I cry at some point during the day each day, wondering if I will be alive to see my children grow up, but what keeps me going is a deep, undeniable faith that everything is going to work out.

I think part of going through any cancer diagnosis is accepting things in stages and taking things as they come. If you try to process it all at once, it becomes too overwhelming and terrifying, especially when you add in the hormones of pregnancy along with a diagnosis. There have been many things I have struggled to accept many things since the time of my diagnosis and throughout chemotherapy. I am getting ready to finish chemo with two sessions left to go, and as I think back on all that has happened and all I have had to accept, it amazes me. If someone had asked me a year ago if I could handle this situation, I would have said no. But I have, and I've thrived. My favorite quote right now, which you will find hanging beside my bed, is by Carl Jung: "I am not what has happened to me. I am what I choose to become."

My first struggle with acceptance was on my first day of chemo. I arrived bright and early to have my PICC line put in first. I didn't cry as it went in, which surprised me. I hate needles. Once the line was inserted, I went to another floor where an x-ray would be taken to ensure that it was in the right spot. The nurse handed me a form to sign, which included a statement regarding the risk x-rays pose to unborn babies. I was seven months pregnant at the time and feeling my little man kick inside me. This was when I broke down in tears. I realized that not only was I going to have this x-ray, but later that day I would be allowing the doctors to pump chemicals into my body, exposing not only me but also my little man to toxins designed to save my life. I sat down on the cold hard bench in the cubicle and cried, holding my stomach and picturing my little man inside me, so sweet and so innocent. I thought about all the diet changes I had made during my first pregnancy and how I had protected my daughter from everything I could: unpasteurized honey, processed foods, and raw fish. I honestly felt like I was a failure as a mother to my son. I was not doing the same for him. I sat there for a long time wondering if I could do this. I emailed Stephanie Brown, my friend and the daycare provider for my little girl, Bronwyn, and asked for a picture of my daughter. She responded instantly. This gave me the strength to leave the cubicle and stand in front of the x-ray machine.

When I entered the chemotherapy lab, my father gave me the strength to accept the drugs entering my system. He reminded me that I was doing this in order to be there for both my children, and they both needed me in their lives. My nurse Katie was amazing; she's a mother, and she double-checked with the pharmacist regarding the safety of the drug during pregnancy. I watched as the drugs slowly entered my veins. My father held my hand and reminded me that all my doctors had told me my little man would be okay, and that my daughter needed me, too. I went through three chemotherapy sessions while pregnant and had to complete thirteen more following the birth of my healthy little Wyatt. The first session was the worst one by far and the hardest one to accept. Afterwards they seemed to become almost routine, just something I had to do.

My second major struggle with acceptance was in regards to my appearance. I'll admit I've always been a little vain when it comes to my hair. My entire life I've had thick long curly hair, which I received compliments on all the time. I viewed my hair as my best physical feature. It started to fall out about two weeks after my first chemo session, right on schedule. Lots of people gave me advice about this. They told me to take control and shave it; don't let cancer take something else from you. I let my friends give me a brush cut and learned that I actually don't mind short hair. It was when this brush cut started to fall out that it became incredibly hard. I remember staring at my hands in the shower, covered in the short little pieces of my hair, and no matter how many times I washed my hair or rinsed it, the hair just kept coming out. My husband shaved it right down, and this was when I started to become self-conscious. I started to avoid going out, using chemo and the risk of infection as an excuse. I would get mad when my husband used video chat with me in the picture without warning me so I could have a chance to cover up. I bought a wig, but it was hot and itchy so I rarely wore it. I tried to own the fact that I was bald and have fun with it. On Halloween, I dressed up as Daddy Warbucks and put my daughter in an Annie costume. We hit up all the neighborhood houses and I tried to present myself as being empowered and confident, but at the end of the night, everyone else got to take their costumes off while I was still wearing mine.

After Wyatt was born, I set up a newborn photo session. This was important to me because we had done it for my daughter, and I didn't want

to miss out on having it done with my son just because I had cancer. I decided I wanted the pictures to look normal. Or in other words, I planned on wearing my wig. We arrived at Kelly Lumley's

place for our photo shoot. My daughter Bronwyn, who was two, would have nothing to do with me and a wig on. As we posed for pictures, she grabbed at my wig and threw it off. She kept repeating "Mommy, no hair! No hair!" As I looked at my daughter and cradled my son, I realized how much they loved me, regardless of my hair. My daughter taught me to love myself regardless of appearance. My appearance would be temporary, but even if it was permanent, I had to accept me for me and where I was in my life. The pictures would be normal without the wig because at this point in our lives, this was what was normal, and I don't believe I should ever hide what I went through from my children. I don't want them to be scared that their mother had cancer, but I'm not going to hide from pictures and have it seem as though I wasn't there for a year of their life while I was going through treatment. I'm not going to change that history for me or them.

I stopped being so self-conscious after that. I'm not going to say it was all roses and that I never felt awkward when someone stared at me, because that's not realistic. But I did learn to accept myself for who I am. I am still carrying excess baby weight, so I might be fat and bald, but I'm still beautiful. Plus, as a bonus, I had been wanting to break up with my hairdresser for two years but hadn't figured out a way to do it. Going bald made it easy.

My final struggle with acceptance was breastfeeding and caring for my newborn once he was here. I breastfed Bronwyn until she was eighteen months old, and she had never spent a night away from me until she was seventeen months. The only babysitters she had were family members and our daycare provider, Stephanie Brown. I loved breastfeeding my daughter. I enjoyed the bond I had with her.

Lying down with her in bed was an amazing feeling, and I'm forever grateful I was able to do it with her. My husband never got up in the night with her, and even when I did go out in the evenings, I always ensured I was home to nurse her to sleep.

I felt cheated with Wyatt. I worried about the bond I would have with him because I couldn't nurse him. I knew nothing about bottle-feeding and sterilizing or different kinds of formula. I struggled preparing for his arrival because there were so many unknowns. I know that breastfeeding is not for everyone, and there are women who can't or who choose not to. I do believe it is a personal choice. I was angry that my choice had been taken away from me. I had an amazing OB-GYN who prescribed a medication that ensured my milk did not come in. I think if I had not been given that pill, there would have been slip ups. I had stopped breastfeeding my daughter when I was diagnosed a couple months earlier, and it just seemed natural to me to want to breastfeed Wyatt. Wyatt did struggle with formula at first, and I struggled with mother's guilt, having to put him on formula. He had constipation and gas issues; however, he is now three months old and thriving at almost eighteen pounds.

Wyatt and I found other ways to bond. I did lots of skin-to-skin time

with him, having him sleep on me for naps with both myself and him topless. I was able to hold his little hand while he was feeding and cuddle him just as much as I did my daughter. Although it's different, I do feel I have as strong a bond with him as I do with my daughter.

Following Wyatt's birth, I still had thirteen rounds of chemotherapy to complete. I thought I was Superwoman and could do the nights with the baby, take care of my two-year-old, and go through chemotherapy. I was wrong, very wrong. I became worn down. I don't know if it's the reason I ended up in the hospital or not, but I am sure it didn't help.

I was diagnosed with febrile neutropenia when Wyatt was three weeks old and ended up spending ten days in the hospital. I had never spent that long away from my oldest, and now I felt as though I was abandoning my newborn baby. I was in isolation, and the doctors did not want the children being brought up to the hospital. I'll admit I'm a bit of a control freak when it comes to my children and the way I want things done. Since being hospitalized, I have learned that I have to accept that things may not always be done the way I want them to be, but my kids are safe, happy, and thriving. And that's all that matters. I had to accept that I can't do all the nights with my son and still get the rest that I need to fight this cancer.

Right now, my mom, my dad, my husband, and I take turns doing the nights with Wyatt. Wyatt, Bronwyn, and I are largely living with my parents because my husband works full-time. At first, I wondered if this would be confusing to them, but it has become the new normal. I'm a social worker by trade and work primarily with children. I always talk about how it takes a village to raise a child and advocate for my clients to reach out and find help where they can. I've accepted that this is something I need to do, too.

I still have an amazing bond with both of my children. Nothing is going to change that I'm their mom—they know that—but because of the cancer diagnosis, I have watched them form an incredibly close bond with their grandparents, aunts, uncles, and cousins that they may not have had if I hadn't been sick. Their great aunt has helped with doctor's appointments, their second cousin has helped when I'm sick, and my sister has taken my daughter for both short and extended periods. Bronwyn has a close relationship with both my parents that I love watching grow. I like to think of Wyatt as being raised by a village of people who all love him. I think this is what has helped me accept the help I need in order to ensure that I get well and beat the beast that is cancer. My treatment will hopefully only be a year long. The bonds and relationships my children are forming now will last them their lifetime.

The key to peace is accepting what you have to and fighting against the rest. Cancer during pregnancy is terrifying, and it changed my perspective on everything. It made me second-guess myself at every turn because I'm not only having to think about myself but also about the life of my child. There are scared moments, there are sad moments, but in the end, it's all worth it because I don't think there is a mom out there that wouldn't do whatever it takes to try to be there for their little one. I remember at my post-natal checkup the resident was screening me for post-partum depression, and she asked, "Do you ever think about dying?" I almost wanted to burst out laughing. Instead I simply said, "If I wanted to die, I wouldn't be sitting in front of you bald."

My next hurdle after chemotherapy is a double mastectomy. I haven't fully accepted that I'm going to lose my breasts. I know I will, and I know that it is part of my road to recovery. I know I can deal with it because I look back at how far I've come. I look at my two amazing children, and I know I have to keep fighting.

Everyone needs to find their own path to acceptance. For me it was largely through my kids and family. I am lucky to also have an amazing group of friends who let me be what I need to be in the moment. I can spill out my fears, I can scream, I can cry, I can tell them life isn't fair, and they will just support me. They don't dump their own feelings about my situation on me, either. I think that's key. Find where you can be you and let your emotions flow.

CHAPTER TWO: HEATHER CHOATE

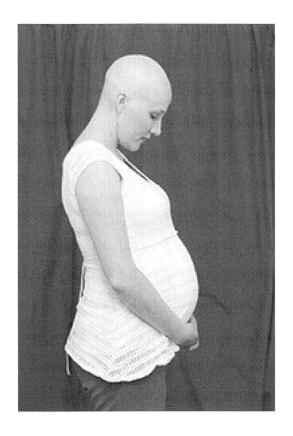

- Diagnosed 17 July 2014 *(10 weeks pregnant)*
- Infiltrating ductal adenocarcinoma
- Four rounds Adriamycin/Cytoxan during 2nd trimester
- Delivered 6 January 2015
- Taxol , radiation, Herceptin, and surgery after delivery

"When I grow up will I be bald like you?" Morgen ran her hand along my smooth, bald head. A reasonable question from a four-year-old. Her older brothers Benjamin, Joseph and Chance were too engaged with a war of Jedi vs. Ogres to bother for the moment. But it affected them, too. Just like it did all of us.

I was twenty-nine years old when I was diagnosed with breast cancer. I was ten weeks pregnant with our sixth child. Yes, six. We may be crazy, but we're addicted to kids. We were thrilled to learn that baby number six was on the way. At my first appointment with the midwife, she asked me if there was anything I was concerned about. For the first time ever, I had to say that there was. I told her I'd noticed a lump on the upper part of my left breast. She examined it and immediately scheduled me for an ultrasound. The ultrasound was followed by a biopsy. All the while, the doctor and nurses told me that it was probably nothing. "You're so young," the doctor told me. "You're healthy and active and have no history of cancer." I took a deep breath. *Of course, everything is fine.*

The following day, the midwife called back with the results of the biopsy. I was on the back porch of our house on a beautiful, warm southern Colorado summer day. The kids were playing in the backyard.

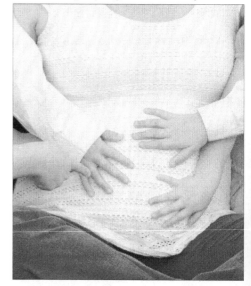

"We got the results of the biopsy," she started, then paused. "Heather, it's cancer."

Everything slowed. The kids running about the yard, the sun falling, my heart. My immediate thought was for my baby. What would happen to her?

My husband and I met a cancer specialist the following day. "I want you to seriously consider terminating the pregnancy," he told us.

"Because your cancer is hormone-fed, the hormones of your pregnancy are making the tumor grow rapidly. It has already spread to your lymph nodes and probably to other parts of your body. If you do not abort, you are risking your life."

Ben and I had made a unanimous decision without a single question or doubt in our minds or hearts before the doctor even told us this. I looked the doctor in the eye. "I would rather die than take the life of my baby."

We were met with nothing but resistance from several other doctors and several friends and family members. "Think about your five children," my dear grandmother told me over the phone. "Benjamin is only eight years old. They need their mother." I understood that they were confused and scared and just wanted the best for us. But I had thought about this, and hearing those words made me want to scream, "I don't have just five kids; I have six. Five born, one on the way. I must think about all of them!"

After days of searching, praying, and studying a plethora of treatment options, we were finally led to an oncologist in Denver who treats young women with cancer and had successfully treated many pregnant women with cancer. We drove the seven hours up from our home in Bayfield to meet with Dr. Borges. She outlined a specific treatment plan for us, informing us that during specific stages of the pregnancy there were certain types of chemo that were safer to take. "It won't be a full treatment, but it will slow the growth of the cancer enough for your baby to be born, and then we'll get you well," she said. We felt peaceful about that option, knowing that God was leading us. We learned of mothers who did this treatment, had their babies, and then passed away shortly after.

That was heartbreaking, but we had to put our faith that whatever happened, God was looking after my baby and me.

Ben was strong for me, but I knew even he struggled. There were so many questions. *Why had this happened? What would the future hold for us? Would I be there to see my children grow? Would they have a chance to know me?* I poured my heart, my faith, and my floundering upon the page. I've always been a writer and writing is powerful therapy, but this time I was writing for something more, I was writing so that if I was taken, I would leave something, so maybe my children and unborn baby could know who I was. I wanted them to understand why I chose what I did.

I had a rattling dream, which spurred me to write, the following, just to get it out:

Last night I dreamed I saw each of my children standing over my grave. It was exceptionally real. I was watching them from across the casket, but they couldn't see me. I wanted so badly to hold each one of them. I felt no pain, but my heart broke in a way that could never be mended. Ben gathered all the kids around and said, "Okay, kids. Now it's time to say goodbye to Mommy."

"What do I say?" Joseph asked, not looking at him, turning his foot in the grass. Through red, teary eyes Ben said, "Just tell her that you love her. You can give her a flower."

Benjamin was crying. He looked a little bit older. Maybe nine years old. He put a flower on my grave and said, "You were the best mom ever. Now I'll never have a mom again." He broke into sobs. Ben held him and let him cry.

Chance stepped up, looking really hard as though trying to be brave. He said, "I have faith that if I choose the right, I'll see you again." He threw on a white flower.

My mother-in-law, Ginger, prompted Joseph forward. He buried his face in her skirt. "Just tell her bye-bye, baby," she told him gently and quietly enough so only he and I could hear her. "Goodbye, Mom," he said in his low, quiet voice.

Morgen twirled in circles a little way off. She wore a pale yellow dress. Her favorite color. She'd gathered a large assortment of flowers, and was singing softly to herself. Ben called her over, "Morgen, come say goodbye to Mommy."

She shook her head but came. Ben knelt beside her as she squirmed. "Do you want to give Mommy a flower?" he asked. Again she shook her head, frowning. She clutched her bouquet close to her chest. "These are my flowers."

"Don't you want to give one to Mom?"

"No."

He hugged her. "Okay. That's all right." He turned back to the grave.

"I do! I do!" Morgen called out loudly.

"Okay. That would make Mom happy."

Morgen took her time picking one out. Finally, she pulled out a pink-and-white lily, one of my favorites. "Here," she said handing it to Ben. He set it on the casket.

"Do you want to give Mommy a kiss?" She nodded. Together, they knelt and blew me a kiss. My mom came next, holding Naomi. She was walking and talking but still so small. "Wave bye-bye," my mom said. Naomi waved her chubby little arm in imitation.

A short way off, my grandmother, Susi, held a beautiful baby boy in a blue blanket. He wasn't even a year old. But he was whole and wonderful. I brushed his cheek and kissed his forehead but couldn't even feel his skin.

I don't want to leave them. Not now and not ever. They are everything to me. I love them more than they will ever know. Tears are streaming down my face. I didn't want to write this, but I have to be true to what I'm going through. It's not all hope and optimism. It's not all doom and gloom.

It's a bewildering, awful, and yet beautiful mixture of both."

Two people told me in the past several days that they admire how strong I am. I don't feel strong. I feel overwhelmed, exhausted, scared, and hopeful at different times. I show a confident face. I cry. I try not to pretend to be anything other than what I am. Am I strong? I don't know. I'm not sure what strength in this situation means. But under all the fear, anger, faith, frustration, there is an unshakable conviction within me that I am doing the right thing. This isn't about me. This is about my baby. The only thing that matters is that she lives. I will do everything I can to protect her. These aren't just words. Sometimes reading them on the flat page can make them so easy to gloss over. "Oh, that's a nice sentiment." That's not the case here. These are the convictions of my soul. They are written into my heart and are stronger than iron and go deeper than a chisel in granite. I will seal them with my actions, with my life. I'm not afraid of pain. I'm not afraid of death. I'm not afraid of suffering. I will do it all, so she can live.

How I handled having cancer with five children

It wasn't easy to deal with the reality of cancer and treatment with five young children. We did our best to be upfront with them about what was happening but to also shelter them from the blunt edge of trauma. During the day, I was still Mom. I answered any questions they had and did my best to be there for them, even when I was often too sick to do anything and Ben came to be home with us full-time.

On June 23, 2014, I wrote, "Yesterday Benjamin said, 'Mom, I don't want you to die.' What do you say to that? We're doing our best to be open and honest with them and explain what is happening in a way they can understand without traumatizing them. That hasn't been easy. They sense the range of emotions from the adults, and I know they are picking up on more than we realize. We took some time yesterday to explain that what I have is serious, but that we have hope and faith. Chance stood up and said loudly, 'I have faith!'"

I made a point to create meaningful experiences with the children as best we could. A highlight for all of us was a whipped cream fight we had. It felt so good to laugh until our bellies hurt. I don't ever want to forget to live like this.

We also involved them in shaving my head. I didn't want them to wake up and see a bald mom! So we had them sit on the counter, and they made silly faces as Ben got out the clippers, shaving cream, and razor blade.

Chance said, "Mom, you look like a dinosaur!" I never thought I'd see myself with a Mohawk, but now I know I can rock that look.

How my husband supported us through it

Ben was my rock. As the fear of chemo and surgery while pregnant loomed over us, Ben and I were both so exhausted. I just wanted to try and forget about it all. Instead, I found myself curled up in a ball in Ben's arms, sobbing. He let me cry and told me it was okay. "You've been so strong," he said. "You've handled

this so well. Just let it out." It was that uncontrollable, ugly cry. But it's what I needed. His faith and unconditional love carried us through. We promise in "sickness and health," but how many of us will remain true when that covenant is tested? Through the incredible difficulties we faced, I learned what true love was.

How we put our faith in God and accepted his will

It terrified me how little control we had over what was happening. It wasn't a problem we could just "fix." The hardest part was learning to surrender to God.

As I went through chemo while my tiny baby grew inside me, I had to trust that everything would be okay, and even if it wasn't, I had to be okay with that. I felt very much like the mother of Moses, placing her child out into the Nile with nothing but prayers and faith that God would protect that precious infant.

God saw us through. He carried us both to safe shores. Kiery Celeste Choate was born January 6, 2015. She was beautiful, healthy, and whole.

We continued to treat the cancer following her birth, struggling through sickness, pain, and weakness that brought us to our knees time and time again. But we found ourselves on our knees in gratitude for one another, for our Heavenly Father, and for His goodness in saving Kiery and I both.

Now, a year and a half later, I am healthy and well, and Kiery is learning to walk on her chubby little legs, getting into everything, and bringing joy into our lives.

We all struggle. We all face adversity and pain in life. I've learned that it's not about what happens to you; it's what you choose to do about it. You must focus on what you want to achieve and not let anything deter you. Change what you can, and make peace with what you cannot. Life is short; none of us knows how much time we have, but life is ultimately good and beautiful and I am now on a mission to share messages that uplift, entertain, and inspire others.

I understand now how important our bodies are and how to nourish them with pure, good nutrition and to feed our minds loving, positive, and radiant thoughts. Love your spouses and yourselves unconditionally. Give love and light to yourself and everyone you meet.

We are meant to shine.

Love and happiness,

Heather

CHAPTER THREE: LAUREN

- Diagnosis: 13 March 2015 (8 weeks gestation)
- Stage 2A triple negative invasive ductal carcinoma, grade 3
- Lumpectomy and node biopsy at 10 weeks
- 4 rounds Adriamycin/Cytoxan, 8 rounds weekly Taxol during pregnancy
- Delivery: 15 September 2015 (at 35 weeks)
- Finished 4 more rounds of Taxol after baby and 30 days radiation

I had looked forward to pregnancy for most of my life. I pictured cute maternity dresses, prenatal yoga, baby bump pictures, and eating all the food I desired. My husband and I had just returned from our honeymoon when I took a test and found out that this dream was coming true! I wasted no time and started Googling about fetal development and pregnancy symptoms and basically pulled all-nighters designing the nursery on Pinterest. I was so excited that I didn't mind any of the first trimester annoyances like having to pee every hour or having sore boobs.

While massaging said sore boobs one night, I was surprised to feel a small hard lump. A sinking feeling set in, and it stayed with me as I made an appointment for an ultrasound and a biopsy. The doctors assured me it was probably nothing to worry about, so I put the lump out of my mind and focused on my baby bump. At eight weeks, I finally had a visit with my OB, and my husband and I got to see our raspberry-sized baby for the first time. Our happiness was cut short when two hours later I received the phone call that I had breast cancer. I was prepared for morning sickness. I was prepared for stretch marks. I wasn't prepared for cancer.

I still shudder when I think about that phone call and the hours and days that followed. I sobbed as I wondered what would happen to the tiny baby I had already grown so attached to. I screamed that it wasn't fair, that I was a vegetarian in great shape and had been doing everything right. I exhausted myself trying to figure out what I did to cause this. I was thirty-three, healthy and pregnant. This wasn't supposed to happen to people like me.

But it did. And I found out in the following days that it happened to lots of young pregnant women. A website called PregnantWithCancer.org displayed stories of dozens of women who were diagnosed with cancer during pregnancy. I connected with a woman from one of my pregnancy apps who was currently going through breast cancer treatment while pregnant. I found a Facebook group full of pregnant, cancer-fighting warriors. And from all these other moms, I found hope.

I realized that I wasn't alone. My cancer mama friends are what got me through some of the hardest moments of my diagnosis. They answered the scary questions that kept me up at night. They gave me the courage I needed to finally shave my head when I couldn't take the clumps of hair coming out in my brush

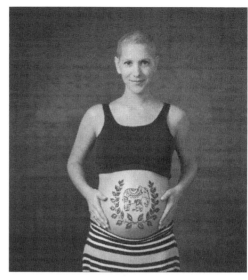

from the chemotherapy. I believe I might have drowned in darkness that first weekend after my diagnosis if it hadn't been for the help of these brave women. They gave me hope that my baby and I could fight cancer together and come out stronger on the other side. I still chat with my fellow cancer mamas daily, sharing tips, answering questions for newly diagnosed women, celebrating our chemo baby birthdays, and giving and receiving hope for the future.

While you will never hear me say cancer is a gift, it *has* taught me to focus on the good things in my life. With every tiny kick, my strong, determined baby reminds me of how lucky I am to have him fighting with me. In my first year of marriage, my husband has become my Superman. My friends and family have encouraged me and made me laugh when I most needed it. I have been overwhelmed with more love than I could imagine, and I am so grateful. I thank my cancer-fighting mamas every single day, and I hope that by sharing my story, I can give confidence to other moms battling cancer or whatever seemingly insurmountable obstacles may be standing in their way. We are all in this together.

CHAPTER FOUR: TIFFANY

- Diagnosed June 2013

- Choriocarcinoma, HCG over 40,000

- No treatments during pregnancy

- Delivered 13 May 2013

- Endometrial biopsy, D&C, hysterectomy (uterus and cervix), Methotrexate 5 days a week, every other week for 10 weeks

I held onto her tiny little hand as I cried. Big fat tears. The kind of tears that build and grow larger and fatter as they come faster and faster. I wept silently in my quiet realization. My mother and husband were unaware, going about their normal business in the next room, preparing dinner. I remember wondering how on earth they could be acting so normal, as if everything weren't falling apart in the very next room, in the chair in which my newborn and I sat. The fact is, they didn't know. My sweet six-week-old daughter didn't know. This was the last time I would nurse my precious baby. Any baby. Ever again. The next day I was scheduled to begin chemotherapy.

I wanted to tell them. I wanted to scream at them. I wanted them to know that this moment was even harder for me than the moment my doctor had said, "Tiffany, you have choriocarcinoma, an extremely rare and aggressive cancer of the placenta. First, we'll perform a partial hysterectomy. We'll remove your uterus and your cervix. Then we'll perform more biopsies to be sure. Next, we'll perform scans to see if there are any other areas of cancer in your body. After that you'll start chemo when we're sure about your diagnosis"

But how could I share this? Who would understand the complexity of the pain this brought? Who could understand the searing pain caused in my mind and heart about something seemingly so trivial when compared

to the possibility of dying from cancer? I was heartbroken knowing I could never have another child, and the pain was worsened through the knowledge that I couldn't even perform the most basic of my duties for this child, my very last newborn.

I've always been a huge breastfeeding advocate. I've talked total strangers into nursing their soon-to-be newborns. My son was nursed for a year, yet I was being forced to give up at less than six weeks with my daughter, the baby I had prayed for for so long and had endured numerous fertility treatments to conceive? I'd had four years to dream about this baby and the ways I would show her my love. I imagined not only nursing her, but doing it for the long haul. I planned to allow her to wean herself, even in toddlerhood if she so chose. How could I give this up? For days I tried to find a plan to get her the liquid gold she deserved. I talked to milk donors, researched the chemo poisons to determine their shelf life, and attempted to find formula as close to human milk as possible. I just could not let go of the thought of nursing her. It was too painful.

I'd done the research. I talked to numerous doctors. Each one told me that nursing her myself was dangerous, which I already knew. The poisons in the chemotherapy drugs would kill not only my cancer cells, but attack healthy cells, too, like my hair follicles. Imagine what they would do to my baby after they were passed to her through my milk. But a part of me thought there was some way I could overcome this and provide my own breast milk to my baby. This research brought me to a Facebook group dedicated to mothers who exclusively pump milk for their babies. "That's it!" I thought. "I can pump and dump my milk until I'm better. This is the solution!" My gynecological oncologist disagreed. "You'll be too sick. You won't be able to keep up. The amount of pumping necessary to accomplish this goal will cause too much fatigue. On top of that you'll be caring for a newborn *and* enduring chemotherapy. No. I don't recommend it." Little did he know, I really, *really* don't like to be told no. On top of this, I was motivated to make this chapter of my life about more than cancer.

I have always wanted to be a mother. I dreamt about a house full of little ones, close in age—one on my leg, one on my breast, and numerous others playing throughout the house. Cancer was taking away my reproductive ability at age twenty-nine. I was not letting it take away the experience of motherhood as well. We'd tried for four years to conceive this miracle. I was determined to raise her the way I had intended from the beginning, regardless of the fact that cancer was trying to interfere.

I resolved to "pump and dump" breastmilk with the plan that I would nurse my sweet Aubrey again after recovery. What did this entail? My research concluded that each twenty-four hour period required eight to

twelve pumping sessions, including overnight emptying of the breast, until she was twelve weeks old. After that I would have to maintain eight to ten pumps a day until she slept through the night. However, even after she slept through the night I would have to express milk at least once between 2:00 a.m. and 5:00 a.m. This would ensure that my milk supply wouldn't drop. However, I somehow had to be able to maintain high caloric intake, drink lots of fluids, and get enough rest if this was going to work. This wouldn't be easy in a perfect world, and I knew it would be particularly challenging when dealing with sickness and long commutes to doctor's offices. I also had a young son entering kindergarten who needed extra attention in these complex circumstances. I couldn't let Brian's needs suffer at all. How could I make this happen? My husband listened to my ideas, as he always does, but I could see in his eyes that he thought I was crazy. He thought this plan was a coping mechanism to get through the diagnosis. He thought this plan was just a way for me to feel like I was in charge of something in my life. I knew this was the resolve of a mother. I had to fight to do the best for my baby, no matter what tried to stand in the way—even if it was something as uncontrollable as cancer. So, he agreed to drive me to chemo each day, ninety minutes there and ninety minutes back, so that I could fit two pumping sessions in during the commute. He would drive and I would cover myself with a blanket and pump in the passenger seat. He would feed the baby in the evening while I pumped, and do the same at breakfast. I would pump while she napped, and I would pump after each night feed. I would also pump while eating and making dinner by using a hands-free pumping bra. We would plan this schedule around the school day, returning from each chemotherapy session before our son would return home. It was going to be a tight timetable. It was going to be strenuous but we were adamant. We had to do it.

At first the plan was as natural as caring for the new baby had been—a few bumps along the way, such as stopping mid-pump to soothe crying or grab a pacifier—but it was working! After a while though, chemo became grueling. Terrible. I didn't want to eat. I didn't want to drink. I was exhausted and overwhelmed by juggling all of this with a baby in tow. I had burns and sores in my throat and mouth, a side effect of the medicine, making it difficult to talk and eat. My energy was sapped. And this is when my husband stepped in. He became a bottle-washing, pump-lugging, bag-packing, appointment-planning, dinner-making, live-in nurse. Each time I needed to pump, he was there with fresh supplies and encouraging words. Each time I was sick, he would care for both of our children, maintain a clean home, and do anything possible to bring me comfort and healing.

Still, the demand grew more complicated. Lack of sleep and the generally unwell feeling led to grouchiness. There were times I had to pull every ounce of energy and will from the depths to make a pumping session happen. I literally had to talk myself into it at times, especially as I began to empty more and more slowly as my breasts grew used to the rented hospital-grade pump. As a result, I began to despise the pumping equipment. Sometimes I couldn't even look at the pump while expressing, so I had to cover it or sit in front of it. Sometimes I hated myself for hating it. It was allowing me to empty my breasts so that I would not dry up.

Without it I wouldn't stand a chance of reaching my goal. I was always in conflict with that pump, yet it was my only hope. I felt at times that pumping was taking over my existence, using up precious hours of my possibly shortened life. There were days I wasn't sure I'd live long enough to make this hurdle worthwhile. I was spending five to eight hours a day expressing milk. Those were eight hours I was not spending with my family, who were all as scared as I was that this time should be spent with them, instead of planning for a future that may never come. I had to take the pump everywhere I went. Every single time. I felt attached to the pump. It was everywhere with me, and I felt that I was constantly pumping. I also had to pay a monthly rental fee, pay for nursing supplies, nursing bras, and nursing pads. However, this money felt wasted because I couldn't give the milk to my baby. I could feel my frustration with the whole process growing.

I soon realized that I had to find an outlet for this frustration or things were not going to progress much longer. I vented to a local mom's group on Facebook and one of them suggested I join a social media group for mothers who exclusively pump breastmilk, instead of direct feeding. This group gave me invaluable advice about power pumping (hour long pumping sessions that consist of pumping for ten minutes followed by ten minute breaks) that saved me on days when chemo driven malnutrition was drying up my milk supply. They taught me how to express faster through massage and compression, and even suggested a technique in which I would lean over while pumping to make the process faster. Their advice kept me going on days when my body wanted to fail and their encouraging words kept me going on days when my determination was wavering.

So, by will and the greatest determination I've ever known, along with the support of my husband and encouraging words from some caring moms on social media, I did it. I pumped and dumped through all ten weeks and five rounds of chemotherapy. After twenty-five chemo sessions, two surgeries, three hospital visits, and roughly three *thousand* ounces of liquid gold dumped into the toilet, we were ready to try

direct breastfeeding again. Our pediatrician was a driven and intellectual supporter, who called specialists and other physicians to double- and triple-check the half-life of the medicine to be sure it was out of my system, along with any harmful effects. We were so proud the day I was given the green light. I remember beaming. I was so proud.

I wish I could say our nursing relationship returned and everything worked out according to plan. I wish my journey ended in successful tears. This is not my story. Those boulder-sized tears I shed before chemo were well spent. That really was the last time I successfully nursed my baby. No matter how much we tried and struggled, my daughter grew to love bottles too much and direct breastfeeding was just too confusing and strenuous for her. We tried numerous contraptions and homemade inventions to assist her in relearning to breastfeed. Bottle feeding is much less exerting than nursing, and once she learned to feed from a bottle, she realized the difficulty in draining the breast, and she would not nurse from me again.

I do have a success story, however. That pump, with which I had a love-hate relationship, helped me produce milk for seventeen months. Thousands of ounces were dumped in the parking lot of doctor's offices, sink drains, and even toilets. But many more thousands were refrigerated and warmed to bottle feed expressed milk to my precious girl. Thousands more were frozen and thawed to provide liquid gold to a nearly two-year-old pig-tailed, cup-drinking toddler. My family affectionately named the precious liquid "mommy milk". Along the way, a few other family members even used the milk on cuts, scrapes, and even wrinkles. Once we even used it to counter the effects of a terrible stomach virus. I spent mornings getting ready for work with a hands-free pumping bra strapped to my chest for close to two hours at a time. I tearfully traded many of my son's tee-ball games to stay at home pumping. After I returned to work I hid in closets and small offices to pump while gulping down lunch and grading papers. I even sat in hot cars, my naked chest draped in towels to hide my pumping from spectators while on a beach vacation. I was attached to my

"milking machine". At one point I even joked that it was my daughter's twin because it had to be packed with care and lugged absolutely everywhere we went.

My daughter may not have gotten her "mommy milk" directly from me, but she did get fresh liquid gold every single day after chemotherapy. And she eventually continued to benefit from this labor by consuming warmed frozen milk for many months after weaning from the pump.

This is what cancer could not take away from me. Pumping was not easy. It was not cheap, financially or emotionally. I hated that pump. Yet, it helped me accomplish the greatest of all goals. My success story is about beating the odds. I didn't just beat cancer, but I took charge of the role it had in my life and the early development of my daughter. I refused to give full control to the disease, instead I changed what I could.

Returning the rented pump was the greatest and worst day. I was certainly closing a chapter in my life. This was the last time I would support a tiny human with my body. No more pregnancies, no more breastfeeding. But I was passing on that special piece of equipment that meant so much to my daughter and me. I hoped that I also passed along my determination to whomever found herself needing it next. I have handed my torch to the next

momma. I don't know her, and she doesn't know me. We are unaware of one another's journeys, but I have said many prayers for her, that her story can end exactly like mine, successful in spite of whatever challenge she may face.

CHAPTER FIVE: DEE

- Diagnosed 14 July 2014 (31 years old and 18 weeks pregnant with first child)

- Stage 3C Invasive Ductal Carcinoma ER/PR +, Her2-, BRCA-, 21/43 lymph nodes positive

- Treatments during pregnancy: Unilateral Mastectomy, 4 rounds of Adriamycin/Cytoxan

- Delivered 20 November 2014 (induced at 36 weeks, C-section)

- Post-Delivery Treatments: 12 rounds of weekly Taxol, 30 rounds of radiation, quarterly Lupron ejections and daily medication (Exemestane) for 10 years, no reconstruction (yet)

W e were almost seven years deep into wedded bliss when my husband and I decided it was time to start a family. Those years were spent in a steady cycle of working and traveling, saving up to take amazing trips to places I'd never been. I wanted to see the world. I'd browse the internet for hours, on a quest to find the best deals on airfare, hotels, train tickets. Planning the perfect getaway became one of my favorite hobbies, and as those years ticked by, my internet savvy paid off: Alaska, New England, Europe. Some of the best memories of my life are nestled within those seven years. But slowly, slowly, the desire to start a family came into focus. We tucked our passports away and decided that 2014 would be "the year of the baby."

It wasn't long before I saw the two pink lines and began what I thought would be a textbook pregnancy. A new adventure! I joined an online group of women who were due to give birth around the same month. Even though I didn't personally know any of these women, I felt a true sense of belonging. We were all on the same journey together, and our little cyber-group was the perfect place to trade information about all things "baby." We complained about weight gain and morning sickness, debated over the best car seat, and envisioned our birth plans. Anything and everything I needed to know about pregnancy was conveniently at my fingertips. Around this time, I felt something strange on my right breast— a hardened area, slightly sore. Once again I turned to the internet, and my fears were quickly dismissed when website after website assured me that changes in the breasts are extremely common during pregnancy. It's almost always benign. *Almost.*

The day that I got the news cancer I was thirty-one years old, and my unborn child was the size of a sweet potato. My textbook pregnancy abruptly turned into a situation my obstetrician had never dealt with before. And my fellow online moms-to-be? I felt like I no longer had anything in common with them. Instead of chiming in about the unfairness of stretch marks and how annoying it was to find flattering maternity clothes, I was suddenly filled with anger that I now had far more serious concerns to worry about. To make matters worse, my older sister learned she also had breast cancer the very same week. The odds of being diagnosed with cancer during pregnancy are 1 in 3,000. What's the likelihood of your sister having cancer at the exact same time? Despite having an army of family and friends gather around in the days and weeks following my diagnosis, I felt incredibly alone.

One night, I stayed awake long after my husband fell asleep, curled up under the covers with my smartphone so the light from the screen didn't disturb him. I was on a mission to educate myself about all things "breast cancer." I learned how it's staged, how to interpret pathology results, neo-adjuvant versus adjuvant therapy. And then I read about survival rates. According to the seemingly reliable website, the five-year-survival rate for stage 3 cancer was 72%. Stage 4 was 22%. I was diagnosed as stage 3, but because of the pregnancy, I wasn't able to completely rule out the cancer spreading, because I wasn't able to have the required diagnostic testing. My mind raced with worry and speculation: Will I be alive in five years?

Careful not to disturb my husband, who was quietly snoozing away, I shifted gears and landed on a website dedicated to young people with cancer. Enough with the somber facts and figures; I was ready to be uplifted with success stories and positive outcomes! I clicked around until I found a section called "Survivor Stories." *Jackpot.* These testimonies gave me hope. They helped me realize that someday in my future, this whole cancer journey would just be a story I tell. I noticed that the website hadn't been updated recently; the stories were a few years old. So, I did a quick internet search to see if there was any recent news about these amazing survivors. One of the first links directed me to an obituary; this particular woman's cancer had returned, and this time she hadn't survived. I searched another name and another obituary popped up. My heart sank and an avalanche of tears erupted as my husband came to the rescue with hugs and reassurance that we were going to be okay, eventually. That night I decided that I would no longer allow myself to slide down the slippery slope of cancer statistics and of comparing my story to other women. My new mantra? "You are your own statistic."

While my internet searching sometimes resulted in added stress and panic, more often it served as an invaluable tool during my journey with cancer. A quick search for "cancer during pregnancy" led me to a wonderful organization (Hope for Two) that connected me with a woman who was diagnosed with a similar type and stage of cancer. We talked on the phone, and I was elated to hear that her "chemo baby" was now ten years old and thriving. Soon I discovered that there were many other women going through cancer treatment while pregnant. I gained confidence in the treatment plan that my doctors mapped out when I learned that it was nearly identical to other treatment plans. I reestablished my sense of belonging when I found a new online community of women who had all gone through breast cancer during pregnancy. Sure, concerns of stretch marks were replaced with anticipation about chemo-induced hair loss, but each and every time someone completed their treatment or posted a picture of their beautiful, healthy "chemo baby," we all cheered and doled out virtual hugs and high-fives. I had found my tribe.

As I continued to process the new direction my life was taking, I felt an urge to start documenting my experience. I started an online blog, and it felt very satisfying to record all of my thoughts and feelings onto (virtual) paper. Not only did this help me keep the chronology of events accurate, it also provided my family and friends with information and updates. I blogged with the intention that it might someday help other women who find themselves in similar shoes.

My tumor was 11 centimeters. I had 43 lymph nodes removed, 21 of which contained cancer cells. If I had waited much longer to start treatment, I'd probably be facing a terminal diagnosis. While clicking around the internet, I found myself poring over breast cancer message boards, looking for people with similar "stats." Trying to find someone, anyone, who had a "bigger" tumor or more lymph nodes removed became an obsession. I didn't find a single person. At first, this was a terrifying notion. Is there really nobody else who has had a tumor as big as mine and lived to tell about it? But as time went on, I stopped looking. I realized that it didn't matter, and I found peace with that. My story belongs to me and doesn't need to be compared to another person's story. I made it through surgery, 16 rounds of chemotherapy, and 30 rounds of radiation. My son is now fifteen months old, and I am here to enjoy him. You can't find that kind of happiness on the internet.

Cancer Mommas Support Group
3 December 2015

Dee "Having my first PET tomorrow. What's the general rule about holding babies afterward? My son is a year old, and I forgot to ask ahead of time about the dos and don'ts. Need to know how long Grandma will have to watch him."

Barbara "I stayed away for an excessive amount for the first one because I was nursing (pumping and dumping for twenty-four hours), but with the second one my kids were one and two and not a few weeks old, so I just stayed away for a few hours. I think maybe I had it and went home and slept and then someone brought them home to bed. Good luck, momma!"

Dee "The main after effect is that you're temporarily 'radioactive' until the tracer dye flushes out your system. So you're supposed to limit physical contact afterward, not breastfeeding, etc."

Jennifer "I've had several PETs at a few different places. Each has a different protocol. I aim for twelve plus hours of no holding/cuddling. I will hug them good night, and so far neither of my children glow. ;)"

Dee "Thanks everyone for the input! Sounds like I can use this opportunity for a midday nap. For the record, the techs just told me no baby holding for eight hours. I guess every place has different protocols."

Jennifer "They also have different protocols about no exercising for a few days ahead of time and what you can or can't eat or drink prior to your scan. My current oncologist is two and a half hours away, and I usually have my scan early in the morning and then stay up there for a few hours to have my consultation with my oncologist in the afternoon and then have the drive home. My hubby goes with and my kids stay with family. I'm not even in the same town as my kids for about eight hours. Praying for calm for you and good results!"

Dee "It's funny how recommendations can vary so much. I was told no exercise the day before and to fast three hours prior (can drink plenty of water though). That's nice you are able to pass the time away from your kids so you're not 'tempted' to break the rule! I should know results Monday, thank you. :)"

Heather "I was told six hours. But that's really the doctor's over safety measures. They told me that the radiation you emit after isn't any stronger than an hour in the sun. And that's like for the first couple hours. It diminishes two times the radiation output by the hour. Put sunscreen on him. . . Haha! Just kidding. Just handle minimally."

Dee "Sunscreen! hahaha! To kill some time, I've decided to take the extra-long way home, with a pit stop at Starbucks. ;)"

Heather "That sounds like a really good idea!"

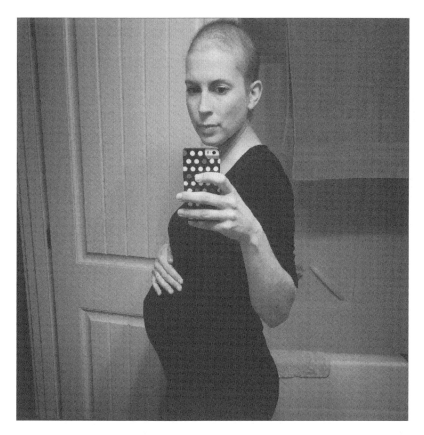

CHAPTER SIX: CAITLIN

- Diagnosed 24 September 2014
- DCIS and IDC left breast, stage 2, grade 3, ER/PR+, HER2-
- Treatments during pregnancy: 2 core needle biopsies, surgical biopsy (considered lumpectomy) 5 rounds of FAC chemotherapy (November-March)
- Delivered 16 May 2015

- Post-delivery treatments: 4 rounds dose dense Taxol, lumpectomy and sentinel node biopsy, single mastectomy and DIEP flap reconstruction.
- Tamoxifen hormone therapy for ten years

Learning of my cancer diagnosis and pregnancy sent my brain into fight mode. I knew I couldn't lose this battle. I was going to do anything to protect this new little life growing inside of me and be around for my family as long as possible. After the initial shock calmed down, I started making a plan. The first thing was to make sure to maintain a sense of normalcy for my oldest daughter, who had just turned two. This was one of the hardest and most important things that I focused on over the year and a half of treatments. At times, it felt impossible. Caring for my family meant something completely different than it ever had before. These are some of the most important things I learned along the way.

I learned how to truly accept help from others. I have always been a get-it-done kind of girl. But this cancer stopped me in my tracks, and I couldn't get things done like I used to. Allowing help from others showed me the abundant support our family had and also helped me learn to ask for help when I needed it. I learned if I didn't ask for or accept help, it was impossible to function. It was impossible

to take care of my family at all. I couldn't let my pride get in the way.

I learned to give myself grace. Grace as a wife, a mom, a friend, or an employee. Letting myself get lost in self-pity or frustration that things weren't normal couldn't last long. I learned to make room for mistakes, for my exhaustion, my frustration and my fear. Allowing myself to feel those things made a huge difference in being the person I needed to be during cancer treatment, especially for my family.

No amount of advice or information read on the internet can prepare you for something like this. Protecting my older daughter was extremely important for me. It's hard to explain what this means. But for us, not discussing cancer with her was the best. At just two years old, she couldn't understand. It was and has been a delicate dance on how to communicate with her when I needed rest or had to recover from surgery. Maintaining a consistent normal schedule for her—and now my younger daughter—has been one of my main priorities. With tons of help from family and friends, doctors' appointments aren't scary. Being gone a lot has been easily concealed with the help of those who walked alongside our family.

Cancer treatment comes along with countless appointments. Add pregnancy to the mix, and it can be overwhelming. Seeing multiple doctors and specialists made my head spin: So much information, and countless choices to make. Already having children at home, a husband, and an unborn baby laid a huge weight on my shoulders to make the best decisions for family. I learned early on how important it is to self-advocate. Ask questions, follow your gut, and don't back down if you feel something isn't right for your family.

Cancer Mommas Support Group
13 December 2015

Caitlin "Would love your input! I know it's so important for us to have the support we need during our treatment, surgeries etc. I've been thinking about the six months – one year after everything is over. I think there is a real need for support still for us. I personally feel like I'm somewhere between: I want to move on with my life but I still want people to remember what just happened. That no, I don't want to talk about my cancer all the time, but I'm not the same and I may still be tired and recovering from chemo, surgery, hormone therapy etc.

My question is: What would be something you would want in that transition time after you are done with treatments? I'm partnering with a local non-profit in my community and feel like I have a grasp on what women need during treatment. But since I'm only beginning the stage of after I'm trying to figure out what is still needed. I hope this made sense and thank you for your input!

For example: Gift cards to get a massage, facial … some type of pampering, house cleaning services, gift cards to Nordstrom's or another store to shop for new clothes, or hand written cards of encouragement."

Barbara "Oh, all of those sound amazing! I am in the after stage. I finished in eighteen months and was done with everything in September. Just now I am starting to feel a ton of energy. A shopping spree or gift card to workout classes or massages would be awesome. Pampering is nice."

Heather "Support in looking good and feeling good. I'm in the after transition and want to gain more energy and lose weight. The brain loss thing is big, too. I'm going to go through chemo rehab to help with some of this, but I think it could help early in the after process. I'm also not sure how to transition with reconstruction. I know I am not finished, but I am reluctant to get restarted there. Just thoughts I guess."

Vicki "An exercise program would be great. Maybe partnering with a gym/Pilates studio/yoga studio, making therapy available, support group with women in the after phase, hair help … a stylist to help with the horrible phase of growing your hair out, and nutrition classes. Just a few of my thoughts."

CHAPTER SEVEN: JENNIFER

- Diagnosed 25 March 2011
- Infiltrating Ductal Carcinoma, grade 3 (high grade), Triple Negative, Stage 3a(T3N2)
- During Pregnancy: Left modified radical mastectomy, 4 rounds Adriamycin/Cytoxan, and 8 rounds of Taxol
- Delivered 13 October 2011
- Post-delivery treatments: 34 daily radiation treatments, 4 more rounds of Taxol

I f I could go back in time and give my eight-weeks-pregnant
self some advice, I would most likely tell myself to stop for a
moment. I was so caught up in the fear associated with my cancer
diagnosis that I rarely stopped to think, to learn, to consider, to reconsider,
and to form my own opinions. I am passionate about education, and I have
seen the difference it can make when a patient is well informed.
Sometimes, when I look back at how I handled my diagnosis and
treatment plan, I get frustrated at my complacency. I desperately want to
go back and shake some sense into my overwhelmed self.

What I should do, however, is tell my past self that it is perfectly okay
to do my cancer my own way. I have learned, and am still learning, that I
have to forgive my past actions and decisions. With all that I now know
about my cancer, I would not make the same choices I made in the past.
The important thing is, neither way would be wrong. It is absolutely
essential to do cancer in whatever way works for, and makes sense to, the
person with the cancer diagnosis.

My husband and I had to make tough choices, with very little time to
think, and we could only hope that we were choosing what was best for
our family. I was told that there was little chance that my baby and I could
both survive. I knew that I could not choose my life over my baby's life.
Two of the closest people in my life wanted me to make that choice. This
was the first, of countless times, that someone else had an opinion about a
treatment choice I made.

If you or your loved one is going through cancer treatment while
pregnant, be ready for your decisions to be questioned and for unsolicited
advice to be heaped on you. For some inexplicable reason, many people
feel entitled to have an opinion about someone else's pregnancy. Those

same people also feel compelled to share that opinion with the pregnant woman, even if she is a stranger. Many of them even feel that they have the right to be insulted if the pregnant woman doesn't have the same opinion.

Cancer patients often get overwhelmed with suggestions from family, friends, and even strangers on what they should be doing and what choices they should be making. I think that hearing about a cancer diagnosis, especially in a young woman, makes people face their own mortality, which can be terrifying. To counter this fear, many seem to think that they should tell the cancer patient what to do to make it all go away. I can't begin to count the number of times I have heard about someone's cousin's teacher's hairdresser who used some random "treatment" to "cure" cancer and now that person is perfectly healthy.

Put cancer treatment and pregnancy together, and you will most likely get either stunned silence or an opinion on what you should be doing differently. Occasionally these suggestions can be helpful. I live in a small town without an oncology department. I found my surgical oncologist and my medical oncologist by asking local friends about oncologists in the city an hour away. The majority of the suggestions I have received, however—especially the unsolicited ones—have been far from helpful.

Each type of cancer is different. Breast cancer is not the same monster as lung cancer or prostate cancer or lymphoma. Breast cancer alone has many different forms. My stage 3a, triple negative, grade 3, infiltrating ductal carcinoma was not treated the same as my friend's stage 1, estrogen and progesterone positive, ductal carcinoma *in situ*. We both had breast cancer diagnosed during pregnancy, but our cancers were unique. Each person is unique and each cancer diagnosis is unique. That's what oncologists are trained for!

Now, I'm going to give you some unsolicited advice: Find an oncologist you can trust. Make sure that oncologist is willing to work with other doctors. Most likely you will have a whole team of doctors working together. I had a medical oncologist, a surgical oncologist, a radiation oncologist, and a high-risk maternal-fetal group that regularly communicated among each other about my treatment plan. My case was brought up at many tumor board meetings.

Make sure that your oncologist is also willing to listen to you. My first oncologist treated me like a real person, not just a random patient. After he moved on to a national position, his replacement did not have that ability. She is no longer my oncologist. You are entitled to an opinion about your care.

Learn about your cancer. It can be terrifying to start that learning process, but the end result is empowering. While I was pregnant, I could not get past that fear. I was told that my type—triple negative—was the best type to have during pregnancy. I was told that the chemotherapy drugs that I would take were safe after my second trimester. I didn't learn much more than that. I chose to bury my head in the sand and hope that the whole cancer thing would disappear when the pregnancy was over. Unfortunately, that is not reality. My metastatic recurrence diagnosis came when I was nine months out of treatment and my daughter was only fourteen months old. At that point, I overcame my fear and learned about my cancer. I am still learning. It is much easier to read my results or have a conversation with my oncologist now that I know more about my cancer. Knowledge is power!

A breast cancer diagnosis brings numerous decisions along with it. Bilateral mastectomy, unilateral mastectomy, lumpectomy, or no surgery? Chemo, or no chemo? Radiation therapy, or not? What order should those be done in? What scans should be done? Genetic testing, or not? Radically alter your diet and  habits, slightly modify them, or just keep doing what you do? If you are informed and can communicate with doctors that you trust, these decisions are much easier to make.

Now that you're under the care of an oncologist, or a whole team of doctors, who you trust and you can communicate with, and now that you know something about your cancer—well, now you are ready for all of the unsolicited advice you are going to be bombarded with. When your neighbor tells you a story about her grandma dying from lung cancer, you will know that her grandma's cancer is *not* your cancer. When your cousin tells you that you should drink lemon juice instead of doing chemotherapy, you will know that you trust your team of doctors and their treatment plan. When your friend asks you if you ate right and exercised enough before your diagnosis, you will know that you did not cause your cancer. When a stranger questions your decision to risk your life to protect the life of your child, you will be able to think about all of the "miracle babies" and their mamas who have survived this process. When someone at your church questions your decision to have chemo while you are pregnant, you will know that many types of chemo are too large to cross the placenta.

Looking back at past actions, or looking from a distance at someone else's diagnosis, it can be easy to say what the "correct" choice should be. Try not to let others do this to you, and try to remember not to do this to yourself. If you are dealing with a cancer diagnosis during pregnancy, or any other trial for that matter, handle it in whatever way works best for you.

Cancer Mommas Support Group
9 December 2015

Jennifer "I took Charlie to a tot gym this morning. It's kinda funny listening to these moms I don't know share their pregnancy and birth 'complaints.' I haven't pulled out the mastectomy and chemo while pregnant story. I haven't pulled out the story of C's little feet hanging out of me while the nurses didn't believe that I was in labor a few hours before her C-section was scheduled for. I'm just sitting here smiling."

CHAPTER EIGHT: BARBARA

- Diagnosed 7 April 2014
- Invasive Ductal Carcinoma Stage 2b, ER+/PR+/HER2-
- Delivered 16 April 2014
- Mastectomy 21 May 2014 with expander
- 4 rounds Adriamycin/Cytoxan, 16 rounds Taxol
- 28 rounds radiation
- Expander exchange summer 2015, reconstruction complete September 2015

C ancer.

Shock. Denial. Fear. Anger. Denial. Perseverance. Elation. Denial. Relief. Exhaustion. Denial.

I nursed Niko for ten months until I found out I was pregnant with George. I was induced with George at thirty-six weeks, after I found out about my cancer. I wanted to nurse him. I got to nurse him thanks to my husband advocating for me, only stopping the day I started chemotherapy. I was on a breast-feeding group that supported one another through the trials and tribulations of

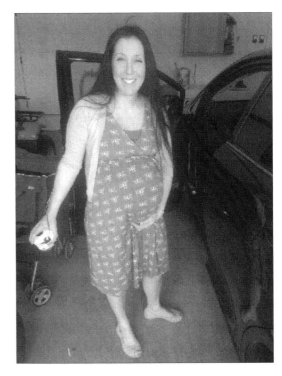

nursing. It was there I shared my story. George was able to receive one thousand ounces of donor milk from over thirty different donors! I had never even considered using donor milk or even knew that was a "thing." It was completely black market. I met women in all kinds of crazy places in order to coordinate pick-ups and drop offs. I was working full time, had two children under the age of two, and fit picking up milk with my giant cooler in the back of my car into our already-crazy life. I knew a few of our donors previously, but most were strangers. At first my husband thought my obsession to provide other women's breast milk to George. But after I insisted that I would never do anything that I thought wasn't the absolute best thing for my child, he came around. He even came with me on several pick-ups. To this day, he says that it was one of the most awkward, amazing things he has ever experienced. These women asked for nothing in return. They were simply providing for my child the one thing that cancer took away from me.

A few of my donors decided to write letters from their perspective:

"George,

I can't remember the first time I met your mom, probably sometime in high school. She was always very outgoing and nice to everyone. She didn't change who she was to fit in or to get others to like her. She was, and still is, a beautiful and genuine person.

When I found out about your mom's diagnosis, it broke my heart. She asked a local breastfeeding group for milk donations. I contacted her right away to let her know I had milk to donate. It was the least I could do. I wanted to help Barbara reach her goal by providing you with breast milk for your first year.

A friend and I stopped by your house one afternoon to drop off some milk donations. At this time you were new to bottle-feeding. During my visit your mom asked if I would nurse you.

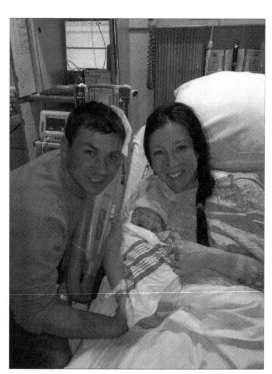

I said yes, of course.

It was my first time breast-feeding a child that was not my own. I knew this was something your mom missed from your relationship. I made sure she was a part of it. She sat next to me, stroking your head while you fed. It was a beautiful moment I will always cherish."

"When I was pregnant with my youngest son due June 2014, I wasn't sure if I would try nursing this time. I had zero experience and about as much knowledge about nursing. So I joined a Facebook breastfeeding support group to try and learn what I could. I decided after being in this group that I would give it a try, 'at least for a little while.' Once I gave birth and he latched for the first time, I cried and a switch in me flipped, and I knew I had to work as hard as I could to give him the best I could. I was very blessed, and it came 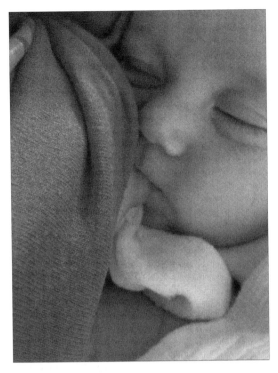 fairly easy for us. But through the support group I learned about other mothers' struggles, and I heard their frustration and devastation when they couldn't produce what their baby needed. It hurt my heart so deeply. Here I was a stay-at-home mom able to sustain my baby and also pump what amounted to a decent little stash. I only pumped in case something were to ever happen, so I had back-up. Then one day I saw a post on the group page from Barbara. Barbara was asking if anyone would be willing to donate any milk for her baby. I read her story and then logged off Facebook. I thought about this, and it weighed on my heart. I thought this poor, sweet mama. She already has so much to worry about. She shouldn't have to worry about having enough breast milk for her baby.

I never even knew or considered the possibility that one could use or donate breast milk until I became a member of that group. I remember the moment I made up my mind. I told God that if I help this mama and give her my milk, I hoped he would continue to help me so that I would never need it. I contacted Barbara and offered her my milk and arranged a time to get it to her. I never regretted that choice, and I actually pumped a little more with her in mind each time or another mother who might need it just in case she never did. I feel so privileged that Barbara let me help, and I gained a sweet friend from the experience, as well. It is a memory that will last in my heart forever. I never knew how much nursing my son would mean to me, I'm so proud that I was able to help another mama out. Even just a little bit."

"Dear Mama,

Hey girl, it's been a while! I have seen your pictures and posts on Facebook that you are expecting. Congratulations! I'm actually due just a few days before you! Isn't that funny, we are both due with our second children around the same time. When I ran into you at your work the other day, I love that we talked about having the same thoughts and feelings about the approaching labor and delivery of our babies. I always get so excited when Mamas share the same views as I do.

Oh Mama, then I find out your diagnosis. Words cannot express how sorry I am to hear this news. Pregnancy is hard enough, but you now have more than the weight of the world on your shoulders. My heart aches for you, and I will be praying for you and your sweet baby. From our conversations, I knew how important breastfeeding your newborn is to you. My baby came just a few days after yours, and pumping was my life for a while, as we had latch issues. I pumped and froze hundreds of ounces of breast milk. The idea came to me, and I never hesitated for a second. I wanted to share the blessing of breast milk with another Mama that wanted to give her baby what she felt was the best.

It is my honor and pleasure to share my love and milk to nourish your baby boy. I look forward to watching your family grow and thrive, bless you all.
Sincerely,
Another Mama"

Amazing mommas.

Amazing experience.

Looking back, I realize Cancer gave and took so many things. It took my innocence, my feeling that the end was not anywhere near. It took my body parts, mutilated my chest, and created physical ailments related to treatment that I will live with for the rest of my life. It took my ability to provide breast milk for my infant child. But it also took my oblivion and turned it into awareness. It gave me strength that I did not know I had. It gave me confidence that there is nothing I cannot overcome through Him. It gave me the beautiful community that I have found through connecting with fellow soul-sisters. For so many reasons and on so many levels I am grateful. Like so many before me and so many still to come, I chose to live happy!

Live happy,

Barbara Vlachos

Cancer Mommas Support Group
8 December 2014

Barbara "Am I crazy if I want another baby? I just got done with chemo, started radiation today. They gave me tamoxifen last week. I am taking it, but I don't want to. I want another baby. Should I just be grateful for the happy, healthy boys we have? Or is there another viable option to have another baby?"

Crystal "I had to have my ovaries removed. We still wanted to have another. But I look at it like this now: We have three healthy children, blessed beyond belief that we were given that gift, and now we plan to adopt. I think even if I hadn't had my ovaries out, because my cancer was all hormone-fed, there is no way I would have another biologically because the risk is so high. Pray about it, and see what your oncologist thinks. It is definitely not worth it if you are putting your life at risk or risking getting cancer again. Hugs to you, momma. I know how much it sucks, but we also have to be thankful we

were given this gift anyways as some women have no option. You are not crazy for thinking or feeling this way at all. Cancer has robbed us all of so much."

Angie "Not crazy. I understand, just need to see if it is possible and pray about it. All things are possible if it is his will with God!"

Amber "Not crazy at all! My Chloe is four months old, and I'm triple negative breast cancer so they say we can try. I also didn't want Chloe to be an only child, but I'm thirty-three and they want me on Tamoxifen for at least three years. Also, chemo has a chance of making us not fertile so I'm aware of that possibility. The way I see it, it's in God's hands! If we're meant to conceive again, we will. If not, it's for a reason! Maybe our Chloe will thrive as an only child, or maybe we're meant to adopt! :)"

Vicki "My best advice is to talk with your oncologist, and also get a second opinion. I hate that cancer takes so much from us."

Tiffany "I had to have a hysterectomy due to cancer and I was completely devastated. You're not crazy. I constantly mourn this loss, even more than a year after the surgery."

CHAPTER NINE: ROBIN

- Diagnosed 22 March 2005
- Breast cancer ER/PR+, Histological grade2, stage 2B, left breast 2 auxiliary nodes positive
- Mastectomy 1 April 2005
- Treatments during pregnancy: 4 rounds Adriamycin/Cytoxan, 4 rounds Taxotere
- Delivered 6 November 2005
- Post-delivery treatments: 35 radiation treatments, tamoxifen
- Prophylactic right mastectomy and bilateral DIEP reconstruction, hysterectomy, switch to Aromatase Inhibitor

My friendship with Daryn has spanned over twenty years. When my hair started falling out in small rat-size clumps, she was the person who shaved my head. Every hospitalization, she sent beautiful flowers. I felt so bad that she was spending so much on me that I ordered her not to. The next trip to the hospital she sent flowered pajamas instead.

During the time I was in treatment, several of Daryn's coworkers were raising funds so they could walk as a team in the Komen Three-Day. This is a bold event where each walker commits to raising $2,300 in order to participate. And as if that wasn't bold enough, at the event itself participants walk sixty miles over the course of three days. All this is done with the hope of eradicating breast cancer from our world. After Daryn's coworkers learned of my diagnosis, they added my name to their 'In Honor Of' shirts. The idea that people I didn't even know were fighting for me moved me deeply. I had never considered doing a 5k walk, much less walking sixty miles and raising thousands of dollars. Things were out of balance and I couldn't leave it that way any longer. I committed to join them in the fight. The following year was my first Three-Day. Every month, I emailed my friends a short story of what it had been like being pregnant and on chemo. I shared my hopes and fears equally and asked them to forward my email to their friends. The result was an outpouring of financial donations like I had never expected. I can't forget the single day where so many people stepped up and over $3,000 was donated. Combine the story of cancer, chemo, and a baby and you can really get people's attention.

The local Early Childhood PTA invited me to be a guest speaker for Breast Cancer Awareness Month. During the opening statement I confessed, "I never did self-exams. I knew I should do them. I simply chose not to." Then I challenged the attendees, a room full of moms with preschool age children, "How many of you perform regular breast self-exams?" The show of hands was dismal. The following year, I was invited to return, and once again I challenged the crowd for another show of hands. There was a complete turnaround. One of the moms told me that I had shamed her in that first show of hands. Like me, she knew what she should do but wasn't making the best choices. She thanked me for being blunt.

There is a huge reason I am drawn to use my voice. Had I been doing regular breast self-exams, I could have found my cancer much sooner, perhaps early enough that I would not have had to subject myself or my baby to chemo. Perhaps early enough that my prognosis would be better than it is. If from this moment forward I can use my voice, there might be some lady within earshot that changes her future based on my encouragement. Perhaps through my fundraising, a drug will be developed that can stop all cancers from spreading. If using my voice and challenging people can have the impact to save just one life, it will have been worth it. I could choose to keep my story tucked safely into a corner, but I choose not to.

I was home recovering from my mastectomy when I heard what was to be Peter Jennings's final broadcast. In a raspy voice, Jennings announced, "Ten million Americans are living with cancer—and 'living' is the key word." It sounded strong, loud, vibrant, and somehow I wrapped his words around me as you would cover yourself with a blanket to protect yourself from an evening chill. It was my mantle. I would focus on the living.

2015

2005

The following year, scans revealed that I had ovarian tumors. Ovarian cancer has some really ugly survival statistics. I was a bit in shock that I was barely out of treatment and with my reconstruction finished, and now I would face a whole new set of issues. Then I was referred to a gynecological oncologist who pulled the rug right out from under me. The likelihood of this being a new cancer was small. More likely this was metastatic breast cancer. Whoa! Back it up! Say what?

It was ten days between that appointment and my hysterectomy. In those ten days, my head went to dark places. I can never erase the journey of emotions from my memory. Metastatic breast cancer meant I would be lucky to see my son, Connor, start kindergarten, and I most certainly would not see either kid graduate from high school. Someone else would teach my kids about the world. Someone else would hold them when they had their first heartbreak. Someone else would celebrate when they got their first job.

In the pit of dark emotions, I looked for light. I sought hope. I have always been told that if you get caught in a riptide and fight it, it just drags you under harder. To keep your head above the water, you have to learn to go with the riptide. So I quit fighting what seemed to be the inevitable and tried to accept this fate with grace. If this was in fact the beginning of my end, one day I would have to look into my kids' eyes and say goodbye. I would have to let them know it was okay somehow. I would have to keep them from fighting it as it

would cause them to drown. But how was it okay? There was only one faint light in that dark pit. I knew I could in fact tell the kids I had done all that was in my power to stay with them. I had subjected myself to every treatment offered. I had gotten off the sidelines and into the fight. I had used my voice to inspire other mommas to take care of themselves. I had been bold by sticking my hand out and had raised thousands of dollars that would advance research in the hopes that their babies would not have to fear cancer. If I had to say goodbye, I would do so knowing I had lived a life of purpose.

The surgery actually revealed the tumor was benign. The removal of the immediate threat did not remove the scars from living in that dark pit of emotions for ten days. But it did cement my commitment to making a difference. My life cannot be lived just so that I have joy and comfort. My life, my voice, and my energy needs to be committed to making a difference. I need to do something! Over the years, "making a difference" has taken on many shapes and sizes. The easy choice is my annual participation in the Komen Three-Day. It is important to me to be raising the money for the drugs I may one day depend upon. But the Three-Day is also cathartic to me. I meet so many fighters that inspire me to do more. So while my participation, coupled with the thousands of other participants, will make a dent in the battle to annihilate breast cancer, in the process I am inundated with three days of love, kindness, and hope that compares to no other experience. To participate in the Three-Day, my "do something" involves hosting a golf tournament/silent auction to raise funds. It has become a big party that grows every year. A couple of years ago, a neighborhood teen was diagnosed with leukemia. The effect this party had on his mom was overwhelming. She saw the overwhelming support from all the attendees as well as all the organizations that donated goods for the silent auction. She was lifted with hope in a time of crisis.

During treatment, the local PTA regularly delivered meals to my family. The ladies came over to care for Connor while I went to radiation. Now I do the same for others. Thanks to Facebook, you can easily find friends and neighbors in need of a hand.

I lead by example, and my kids follow. My daughter Rachel has a "do something" in her heart. She started "Cheesecakes for a Cause" and sells homemade cheesecakes, and the funds collected go to a seasonal cause. She has donated thousands of dollars to an elephant orphanage, to Christmas Child and Angel trees, and to a neighbor that was raising funds to cover the cost of adopting a child.

My "do something" took the form of counseling newly diagnosed cancer patients on treatment options, how to deal with side effects, how to choose surgical options, and how to cope with the search for a "new normal." Whether breast cancer or any other form of cancer, I help people to seek out the experts in the field of diagnosis. I encourage them to interview doctors and seek second opinions. After seventeen years of struggling with lupus, my forty-six-year-old friend was told there was nothing more the doctors could do but keep her comfortable. Hospice recommended moving Cindy to a nursing facility where she could receive continuous care, but she would be away from her children. Instead I promised Cindy that whatever it took, she would die at home with grace. I created Cindy's Angels, ladies who each committed a few hours every week to care for her. It was often scary and uncomfortable, but in those times, I would put myself in

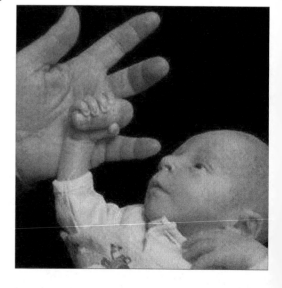

Cindy's shoes and realize that I had little to fear and only love to offer. We

were Cindy's angels, and now she is ours. What is your "do something"? There is power in the word *yes*. Say yes to your challenges. Say yes to the mountain you must climb. Let your journey be larger than your own story.

CHAPTER TEN: HEATHER T

- Diagnosed 18 June 2014
- Triple negative infiltrating ductal carcinoma, grade 3, stage 2b, BRCA1 +
- Treatments during pregnancy: double mastectomy with reconstruction, exchange and 4 Adriamycin/Cytoxan

- Delivered 27 March 2015
- Post-delivery treatments: 12 Taxol, 4 Carboplatin

Life doesn't stop for cancer and cancer doesn't stop for life, so I had to figure out how to do both. At the time of my diagnosis, I was in the middle of buying a house, throwing my daughter's birthday party, selling my mother's home, and planning a wedding. I had a busy life as a single mom, Girl Scout troop leader, and full-time guidance counselor.

Before cancer, I acted like I was Superwoman. I handled my busy life with my cape on, helping people around me in every way I could. Little did I know I'd be turning my cape around into a bib so I could be served.

When you are a helper, you spend your life serving others. It's really hard to stop doing that role, let alone have it switched around. But there I was in the middle of buying a house and the rest of life, and then I'm hit with a breast cancer diagnosis. I kind of knew this was more than I could handle on my own. Little did I know of all the help I would receive.

I knew what having a mastectomy would do to me. I had helped my mother when she went through it, so I knew I'd be helpless for at least two weeks straight. For the first week I'd need assistance with everything, including washing my hair and changing drain tubes. I knew I had to schedule my move first and somehow get settled in my new home before the mastectomy. I had to reach out and ask for help. That was the hardest part of all this. I didn't really know how to ask for help.

I talked to my small group at church and asked for prayers, as well as help moving if they were available. I knew it would be a stretch. It was summer, and people were on vacation. I reached out to friends and family as well. A week before the move, only about four people had committed to help. I didn't know if that would be enough, but I prayed to God and fully put my trust in Him at this point. I'm not sure I'd ever done this in my past. I was floored at the response to my prayers.

The volunteer coordinator at my church called and said to hire a moving crew, and the church would pay for it. I hired two more hands to my crew. I figured we could really get a lot done with that help.

The most amazing thing happened next. On August 2, 2014—moving day—sixteen more people came out of the woodwork to help. Friends, family, church family, and co-workers and their family just showed up to help me move and unpack my belongings into my new home so I could be settled in and prepared for my mastectomy four days later. I was so amazed and humbled by the amount of help I received.

As I look back on the move and the surgery, I realize that the timing of it all could not have been planned better, and I can take no credit in this plan. I thought I was moving closer to my work and my fiancé's work. Instead I moved right into the heart of where I would find the most support. Lord knows I wasn't expecting that at all. My intention was to move closer to where I serve. Not to move closer to be served.

Let's just throw a little something special into this mix. Two days before my mastectomy I found out that I was pregnant. My fiancé and I were shocked. This was definitely not planned and not exactly good timing. But we both wanted a child together, so it was very good news. I had thought that with the BRCA diagnosis and my age (I was thirty-seven at the time), that it would mean I would also be having my ovaries removed soon after the mastectomy. Recommendation for BRCA1-positive women is to have ovaries removed before age forty because of a high risk of ovarian cancer. Well, that would have to wait now. There was going to be a baby instead!

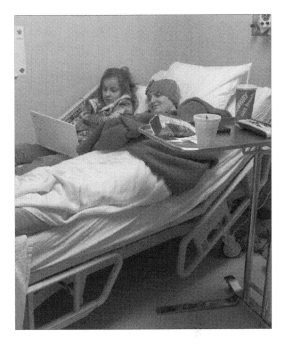

But what did being pregnant mean now? How was that going to affect the cancer and the surgery? The good news was that my cancer wasn't being fed by the hormones I had from being pregnant. My general and plastic surgeons said I could still have surgery, but it meant a possibly higher risk of miscarriage at that early of a stage. I was four weeks pregnant at the time of surgery. They were going to change some of my anesthesia a little, and I had a small amount of radiation injected into me to help determine staging of the cancer. All of it came with a risk, but the risks were much smaller than the benefit. We moved ahead with the mastectomy and prayed for the safety of the baby.

After the mastectomy, I needed a lot of help, and I had to plan it out a little beforehand. The mastectomy would mean I wouldn't be able to lift my arms over my head, I could lift very little weight, and I wouldn't be able to care for myself, let alone my eight-year-old daughter. I knew I needed help, but I didn't know how to ask for this kind of help, and I didn't know how to coordinate it either.

I spoke about my concerns with a co-worker who heard about my diagnosis on Facebook. She suggested an online volunteer site called VolunteerSpot. She helped me set up the site for the dates I'd need care. Personal care, meals, and care for my daughter were all arranged there. I sent out emails and Facebook posts to ask for help. I asked that my family and close friends help me with personal care since it was, well, very personal.

If my mom were still alive, she would have been right there with me, but I didn't have her anymore. Thankfully I do have a really close friend who isn't squeamish, and she stayed with me the first couple nights home. I'm also lucky to have a couple of cousins who are nurses who came from two hours away to stay with me. My aunties, who cared for my mom before she passed away, also came to care for me. My fiancé also proved to be a caring support as well. I'm a very blessed person with all the people in my life, to say the least. As my caregivers came, I got to explain to each of them that I was also pregnant. It was happy news in the midst of

a cancer diagnosis, and it gave me so much more to live for.

After I recovered from the mastectomy, I went back to work. I made it back just in time for the first day of school and to start training an intern as well. I also had to work on selling my mother's home and planning my wedding. But at my first pathology visit with my surgeon and my first visit with my oncologist, I found out I had stage 2b cancer. I had to have chemotherapy, but I had to wait until my second trimester since I was so early in my pregnancy.

I explained my situation to my realtor about my diagnosis and pregnancy, and he pitched in and helped me get my mom's home ready to sell by helping me coordinate contractors and painters and the floor installation. He was a great help and I am forever grateful for his services to me.

My intern was awesome. She came with a lot of teaching experience, so moving into a school counseling role was very easy for her. She helped me with a lot of work tasks, which allowed me to get ahead on a lot of work that year. My intern was with me for just two short months. She knew what I was up against with my job and my diagnosis. As the weeks went by at work, it was becoming more and more of a reality that I might not be able to stay through the year. I had to start chemo in my second trimester. If I took off work after I started, I would have had to go through three months with unpaid leave before my long-term disability would kick in. I didn't know how I would pay my new mortgage and the rest of my bills without my income. Again, I was ready to just give it to God. It was then that my intern astonished me.

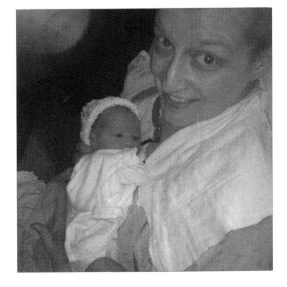

She asked me if she could throw me a benefit so I would have the money to pay for the doctor bills and cover the time that I would be at loss of an income. I honestly didn't know how to say yes to this. It was beyond anything that I could even ask for, but somehow, I said it. I said yes to help.

She collaborated with my co-workers and my small group at church to put on a wonderful benefit. I was shocked at all those who came and contributed. I don't think I can even recall all the people who did. It was very humbling.

I couldn't tell you why or how things happened, but help poured in. The benefit raised enough money to pay the bills for those three months without pay. I was not expecting this at all, and it started an avalanche of help.

Someone tipped me off to a program called Cleaning for a Reason that provides free house cleaning while undergoing chemo. A local cleaner was connected to me and provided four whole-house cleanings. It was very nice.

My dad took me to all my chemo appointments, and I was grateful for that. We really had a chance to spend some quality time together. Since he is retired, he was the perfect person to help with that. It helped that my move put me closer to him, so it wasn't a burden for him.

After the benefit, help just kept coming. As I prepared for a new baby with little extra money, I couldn't afford much. Since it had been so long since I had a baby, I no longer had baby stuff from my first child to reuse. I didn't expect a shower for a second baby, so I never let anyone plan one for me. I had little for this miracle on the way. But help came in that area, too. People donated gear like cribs, strollers, and car seats. I had boxes and boxes of gently used baby clothes in sizes that would keep the baby clothed for over a year. Friends, family, and so many people around me pitched in and kept bringing gifts. I was overwhelmed with gratitude.

Asking for help didn't stop there, either. After the baby came I had six weeks to prepare for my next round of chemo, which was going to require more help with the baby, the meals, and someone to take me to chemo. I used VolunteerSpot again to allow others to sign up for tasks to help me. My dad kept taking me to weekly chemo appointments and down the road many other appointments for shots. So many people from my life pitched in with baby care, meals, and household chores.

It's certainly not easy asking for help dealing with cancer, especially if you are used to being the one who is the helper. The perspective it gave me to be helped by so many during this time in my life made me realize how important the role of a helper is. Not only do I appreciate others' help

in my life, but I also realize how important it is to help others as well.

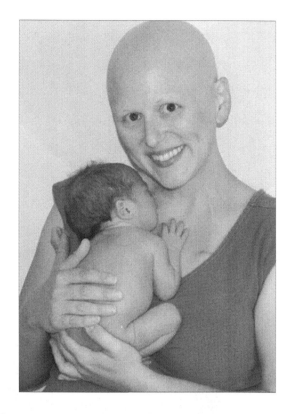

CHAPTER ELEVEN: STEPHANIE

- Diagnosed 30 March 2015
- Invasive Ductal Carcinoma, stage 2B
- ER+/PR+/HER2+
- Lumpectomy 15 April 2015
- 6 Adriamycin/Cytoxan while pregnant
- Delivered 7 August 2015, cesarean section
- 4 Taxotere/Herceptin post delivery

- Bilateral mastectomy and tissue expanders 19 November 2015
- Radiation 25 rounds, breast reconstruction, radical hysterectomy, 10 years aromatase inhibitor

We call it the cancer monster. We wanted the boys to understand and be fully in the know of what was going on, but we also didn't want them to be afraid. My husband and I discussed how we would tell them. "Something inside Mom is trying to kill her, but we think the baby will be okay"? Nope, too scary. After a lot of tears and prayer we decided to tell them something they could understand and grasp at their age, while still being completely honest about the situation. Our boys know superheroes, villains, and Teenage Mutant Ninja Turtles, so that's where our story began. We drove the boys to get ice cream, which is what we do when we want to have serious talks with them. Keep in mind our oldest was seven at the time. Our conversation went something like this:

Mom Hey boys, we need to tell you something really important.

Boy #2 [Boy 1] is touching me.

Dad Boys, no touching each other. We want to talk about something and we need your listening ears on.

Mom I went to the doctor last week to have some tests done on a little hard spot on my right breast. They said that some of my cells have mutated, and the mutant cells are growing fast and trying to take over. Cells are itty bitty building blocks that are inside our bodies that give us life. They call the mutant cells "cancer." We can call it the "cancer monster" if you'd like.

Dad Have you boys ever heard of cancer before?

Boy #1 Yes, I've heard of cancer. Is Mom going to die?

Dad Some day we all die, but Mom is not going to die for a long time. Mom's little cancer monster was caught early, and the doctors say that they can fight the monster and win.

Mom Fighting this cancer monster is going to be hard, but I know that we can be strong. I will need to have a surgery to cut the core of the cancer monster out. After that I'll need something called "chemotherapy"—or they call it "chemo" for short—to shrink and kill any remaining mutants hanging out in my body. When I have my chemo, a lot of my good cells will also die, and that will make me weak. It's going to make me very tired and it might make me sick, too, but just know that when I am sick or sleeping a lot that means that I'm winning and the cancer is dying.

Boy #2 Will the baby get sick too?

Dad Your mom has lots of great doctors that will check on her all the time to make sure that she and the baby are doing fine. The baby has a protective shield around him, like a force field that will keep him safe during her treatments.

Boy #3 I'm hungry. I want to go home.

Mom Okay boys, let's head back home. You can talk to Dad or me anytime you have a question about what's going on. You need to know that there are a lot of different kinds of cancer, and some people die from cancer. You might have friends that tell you about

someone they know who has died from cancer. I am not going to

die right now. I am going to have this baby, and we're going to have lots of fun and adventures still, but this summer won't be like what we planned. We need to all practice a little more patience while I fight the cancer monster. Thank you for being good listeners. I love you.

That was it. We made it through without crying, without making them afraid. Most of the conversation was said with a smile and a confident voice. I think angels were with us, helping us be strong. Up until I had my surgery, I tried very hard to be brave for my boys, but there were many tears shed. Hugs were a little longer than normal, and snuggling time was mandatory for our sanity. Cancer conversations came up frequently because so many adults wanted to talk to us about it, often in front of our children. I was so grateful for those friends and neighbors who were able to have an educational conversation in front of my kids without crying or scaring them with worry. Children are always listening, even when you think they are busy. Their minds are like little sponges, and my husband and I were glad to be able to teach them about cell growth, the immune system, and anatomy. We decided to make surgery and chemotherapy a celebration of winning a battle against the beast. We collected and purchased small gifts and activities for the boys that we called "chemo gifts." After each treatment, I would surprise the boys with a gift bag filled with their surprise. They would get excited, and it was a great distraction while I was in bed for a few days. The excitement of the celebration was so great that on my last chemo, they were actually a little sad that there wouldn't be any more chemo gifts.

I was always very grateful for all of the talks we had with our kids about cancer. It's something I wish they never had to learn about, like war or hatred. We taught our boys that *hate* was an unnecessary word and should rarely be spoken, but during treatments I told them that I hated cancer. I wondered at what age a child stops being a child. I learned that the child is always there even in old age, but little pieces of maturity and awareness bloom through time from experiences. Cancer has aged my family, and it has grown us closer together. Over time my young boys will forget many—maybe all—of these moments with my cancer, but their empathy will remain. I hope they can take the best of what they have learned and what they have seen in the service of others to our family and grow into the men that God intends them to be.

Cancer Mommas Support Group
15 May 2016

Stephanie "There is so much that cancer takes from us, but cancer also gives us a new perspective and appreciation for life. What has cancer given you?"

Barbara "I believe that cancer has given me way more than it has taken from me. I have noticed a tenacity and grit that I haven't seen in myself for a long time. I have more love for this experience than hate. I stand taller and walk more intentionally than I ever have before. My cup overfloweth."

Heather "Cancer has given me a new perspective on life. It's helped me appreciate what is most important. It's given me a sense of humility."

Diana "Cancer has brought some amazing people into my life, I've forged new friendships that I have no doubt will be lifelong."

Heather C "I feel like I have a second chance at life now. I've lost so many of my old anxieties, fears and heartaches and in their place, I have this hunger for life and an unstoppable drive to be the best me possible. I don't let anything, including myself, hold me back. I'm pursuing my passions with a vigor because life is too short to play small!"

Caitlin "Cancer has given me a new perspective in every aspect of life. It has given me a greater empathy for others going through traumatic events. Cancer has shown me the beautiful support network in my community and has given me a clear view of my passion in life: giving back to other women going through breast cancer."

Allison "I would say that cancer has given me a new spectrum of judging what is *really* tough or difficult in life, and what qualifies as 'no big deal.' I can let some things go easier and hopefully see the bigger picture a little more clearly. I also feel like the ladies I have met on this journey have been a great blessing to me. I have been inspired by others, and I understand what it means to love someone just by serving and being there. I have a new understanding of depression and how debilitating and exhausting it is. This is a good thing because I understand others who struggle better now and also want to help other post-treatment ladies who are suffering."

CHAPTER TWELVE: AMY

- Diagnosed 25 November 2013

- Invasive ductal carcinoma, stage 2B/3A

- 17 December 2013 lumpectomy and auxiliary node dissection

- Treatments while pregnant: 4 Adriamycin/Cytoxan, 4 Taxol, at home Neupogen

- 1 May 2014 Lumpectomy

- Delivered 22 June 2014, induced at 37 weeks

- 30 radiation treatments, 5 years Tamoxifen

I blinked in disbelief as the line began to form. Impossible. I had definitely wanted this, but now that proof was staring me in the face, I could feel a wave of panic creeping in.

Anxiety comes from a lot of places. I'm an older mom—to some, a *much* older mom. I've had my hopes dashed more than once. I was blessed enough to give birth to a healthy son at age forty and never imagined myself wanting more than one child. Until I did. And from the moment I was able to admit this inconvenient truth to myself, the two halves of my brain, the logical and the emotional, joined in conspiracy against me. "You are far too old for another child. You are greedy. Selfish. Karma will catch up to you."

Some context: The younger version of myself contained *zero* maternal instinct. As the baby of nine kids, I watched my mother tirelessly slave, day in and day out, to care for her massive brood. I was still in elementary school when my three sisters walked down the aisle, young brides quickly morphing into young mothers. This was life's pattern, how things were meant to be. A world swaddled in stability. To some, comforting. To me, suffocating. Indistinguishable from conformity. A slow, stale, choking death-by-minivan life of PTA meetings, house payments, and crappy part-time jobs. My mind was set. I promised myself I would *never* fall prey to the trap.

At age twenty-one, I left my small New England town and headed to California. At age thirty, I moved to Paris, France, to marry a man I'd met just six months prior. And by age thirty-three, I was filing for divorce and returning to California, financially broke and emotionally broken.

Ironically enough, it was that whirlwind relationship that awakened my dormant biological clock. I had finally felt ready for marriage and family, but my admittedly dramatic attempt fell flat. I found myself more emotionally drained than ever, with a gnawing whisper of "hubris" in my ear.

At thirty-seven, I met the man who would convince me that this marriage thing was worth another try. After two years of adventurous courtship, we got engaged, and I was shocked at just how quickly and easily my "old eggs" came through with a pregnancy.

I was elated. We weren't yet hitched, but 'twas a small detail. The wedding would take place at fifteen weeks' gestation, and I would use that venue to announce the happy news. But that was never to be. At eleven weeks, during a doctor visit for some routine testing, there was no longer a heartbeat. A D&C procedure followed, and months of mourning set in. I feared I'd never have another chance.

During that time, obsessive thoughts crept in. I'd screwed around so long. Made so many mistakes. Spent so much time chasing down improbable dreams with impossible men. And it was now time to face those consequences. I spent so much of my young life trying *not* to get pregnant, and now that I was ready, my body was betraying me. There was a distinct possibility that my time was up, and I'd have to accept my fate.

I spent weeks and months crying, reading through blogs and Googling "pregnancy at advanced maternal age." I became intimately familiar with the odds: Notwithstanding fertility treatments and interventions, a woman at age thirty-nine has very low chance of getting pregnant within X amount of time. I turned those numbers over and over in my mind. I charted, I vented online to women in pregnancy loss groups, I obsessed on my odds. Nothing else mattered.

And then it happened. Six months later, the lines again turned blue. And after an uneventful nine months, I gave birth to a healthy baby boy. He was perfect: chubby, dimpled, sweet, and easygoing. Impossible not to love. I took to mothering like I'd been born for it. And almost immediately, the unexpected happened. I started feeling a twinge of jealousy around my younger girlfriends, the ones who were already talking about their next pregnancy. I would get excited for them, then feel a flicker of regret. Did I dare? How could I even hope? Having one child after forty seemed like a small miracle; having two would certainly be pushing my luck.

Following a lot of teasing and halfhearted threats between hubby and me, my mind was made up. We would try again. I figured it would never work, but hey, might as well give it a shot. After all, I had nothing to lose.

Fast forward to November 2013. It's a few short weeks before my son's first birthday, and I'm sitting at my desk when my nose spontaneously begins to bleed. Huh. Strange, but not scary. Figure it must be dry sinuses, allergies, whatever. Hubby is brushing his teeth, and when he looks over and sees me Kleenex-faced, he drops the toothbrush and asks, "Has your period come yet?"

"No, why?"

"You know that's a symptom of pregnancy! Take a test!"

So here we are. Again. Staring at the blue lines, incredulous. I am simultaneously giddy and freaked out. Could this be happening? Would this one be viable? Can I really do this again? And then the other, more sinister voice chimes in: "There's still that lump. You know, that one you've been ignoring. Assuming it was a blocked duct. A cyst. Some mix-up in your breastfeeding plumbing."

I'd stared at it more than once in the mirror—a strange, rounded protrusion under the fleshy part of my left breast. It had been there for a while. Had it grown? Hard to say. Did it bother me? Sometimes it sent out strange shocks, like a hot flash of electricity. Hard to describe, but intense. This was part of the reason I'd always dismissed it as an unfortunate by-product of breastfeeding. Must be some low-grade mastitis. Uncomfortable, but certainly not going to kill anyone. Once I weaned my kiddos, Lefty would shrink right back down to her normal size, and life would carry on.

Two weeks later, I am lying in the stirrups at the OB's office. Everything looks great. Heartbeat is present, tiny creature measures correctly. Sigh of relief. As I pull up my pants, I casually mention, "Hey, there's also this lump. Would you mind having a look?"

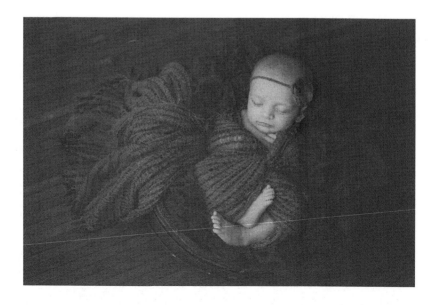

My OB nods. "Sure, no problem." I lie back down and she runs her hands over my breasts—first right, then left. I watch her face for signs, and take note as her brows furrow intently. Her expression is straining to stay neutral. My stomach sinks a bit.

After asking me to sit back up, she calmly explains that she wants me to have this checked. In fact, she is calling the hospital right now, to see if they can do an ultrasound and biopsy this afternoon. I protest. Today is no good. I snuck away from my desk without mentioning why. I need to get back to work before anyone notices my absence. She sits me down and stares into my eyes. No. This is serious. You need to clear your calendar and be seen. Today. *Right now.*

Cue freak-out. I'm forced to pull myself together and phone my boss. I tell her about the lump, dismissing it as no big deal, but something I wanted to have checked out. I hear her voice falter a bit. She agrees and reassures me that it's probably nothing, but yes, certainly best to have it checked. Then, after hesitating, she adds, "Hey, listen. Even if this *is* something, just look at me. Twenty years out, and I'm still here!"

"What do you mean? You've been through this?!"

"Yes. Double mastectomy. Don't worry; no matter what happens, life will go on." I thank her and hang up, sick with worry and with the deception of having concealed the bigger half of the story.

A long weekend passes, during which we host a first birthday party for our baby boy. I distract myself with activity. Say nothing to my friends. Put on a brave face, and wait for news from the doctor.

On Monday morning, I get the call. It's official. I have cancer.

The next forty-eight hours are a blur. Phone calls to and from doctors. Family. Close friends. So much uncertainty. I feel altogether doomed.

There is no way this pregnancy could ever result in a healthy baby. And worse yet, I know that I will be forced to make that call—that incredibly painful call—to decide what was more important, pursuing aggressive treatment or continuing the pregnancy. I've always been a staunch advocate of a woman's right to choose, which in my particular situation was proving to be sickeningly ironic.

In all this darkness, the only hint of light reflects from an organization called Hope for Two. In my desperate consultations with Dr. Google, I stumble upon their site. It's a non-profit run by and for women in my exact situation. I pore over stories of patients who have gone through cancer treatments while pregnant, survived and given birth to healthy babies. Pages and pages of photos. Bald heads and big bellies. Happy moms, happy babies. Their smiling, beaming faces gazing back at me. Maybe not all is lost. I find the contact number and make the call. A very sympathetic counselor responds, reassuring me that I will be put in touch with a support woman and an MD consultant who will reach out to me immediately. I regain a tiny bit of positivity. Maybe I'm not totally screwed. Maybe this could work out.

Two never-ending days after receiving the news, I finally meet with my assigned team of doctors. Most had not dealt with any such situation before. One of them—the oncologist, no less—pretty much blurts out that I will have to terminate the pregnancy, that it would be foolish and selfish to think otherwise. Her gloomy outlook throws me right back into a funk.

Thankfully, just as soon as she walks out of the room, leaving me in shock and tears, two other doctors, a surgeon and a perinatologist, come in. They ask how things are going, although my face tells the whole story. I relay the news that the oncologist has just told me. I can see their expressions change, harden a bit. They seem protective. Reassuring. They talk me down from the ledge. They rally behind me. They make it clear that if I want this baby, they are going to back me up one hundred percent. They are my guardian angels, and given their blessing, I feel strong enough to proceed.

As the first order of business, they assign a new oncologist to my case. Then they schedule my first surgery, a lumpectomy, to happen just a few weeks out from diagnosis. And my chemo is timed to begin as soon as I hit fourteen weeks gestation.

My treatment plan is aggressive, but proceeds like clockwork. My consulting doctor, Elyce Cardonick of Hope for Two, reminds me constantly: "Insist upon being treated as though you were not pregnant. Don't let them skimp on anything out of fear for the baby's health."

So we don't hold back. Dose-dense chemo every two weeks? Check. Neupogen injections between treatments to keep my blood counts high? Check. Constant visits to different doctors, to monitor the baby's health and my own? Check. Time flies past. Once the chemo is complete, I have a second surgery to clean up the margins. I am then cleared for delivery, a scheduled induction at thirty-seven weeks.

My first pregnancy was so normal, so uneventful. This one is anything but. Things happen so quickly that I don't have time to feel sorry for myself. I admit to having some sleepless nights and to fretting about the baby. A whole army of folks fret about us both, but in truth, I respond very well to treatment. Hardly any nausea, side effects largely manageable. My hair falls out as my belly grows. I learn to tie colorful turbans and pencil in convincingly accurate eyebrows. I keep myself very busy between work, doctor appointments, caring for a toddler, and readying a rental property for sale, and before I know it, we are checking into the hospital to give birth to our little miracle.

Of course, every baby and every birth is special, but I can't help but smile when I recall the words of a dear friend and former professor when I described my predicament. After recovering from the universal "*Holy shit!*" reaction, she chuckled and said, "Well, you have never been one to do things halfway. Whatever you do, you do *big*."

And for once, this feels like an understatement. This battle, this pregnancy, this baby: This is *big*. This child who happened so unexpectedly, who saved my life. The baby girl I thought I'd never have. My perinatologist, an in-demand specialist with a huge caseload, very rarely attends a birth, but she drops everything just to be there for my delivery. The residents fuss over me and fight on my behalf to perform an on-site tubal ligation. When it was offered to me, I was only too eager to take them up on it. Quick and easy, one day post-partum? Sign me up! Now that the day had arrived, there was a glitch. Bureaucracy. Apparently, the hospital doesn't do this routinely. Not enough attending staff, not a priority procedure, too much hassle. So I accept the news, tell them it's okay, I don't want to put them through so much trouble. But they are having none of it. "You have been through enough. We are *not* letting you leave here without that tubal!" And as promised, they get it done. The nurses on staff are so amazingly attentive and kind. Doctors and administrators drop in to see me and to meet our little bundle. We are mini celebrities in the labor and delivery wing of Kaiser. Our family is surrounded by love and positivity. The planets have aligned and bestowed this little blessing. Mira, our incredible little miracle, was destined to be mine.

It's been nearly three years since our crazy journey began. I'm now forty-four and a cancer survivor. Hair has grown back, scars mostly healed. Aside from the tattoos I have chosen to commemorate my battles, I look pretty much like any other tired, harried, normal mother of two young toddlers. I still refuse the lure of the mini-van, but have compromised with a shiny red SUV. PTA meetings are still in the distant future, but we did

just buy the big suburban dream house, complete with a dog, two cats, a big yard, and an even bigger mortgage. And you know what? I'm more than okay with that. In Cancerland, stability is not a dirty word; it's a blessing. And I for one have learned that we need to acknowledge and accept life's blessings as they come.

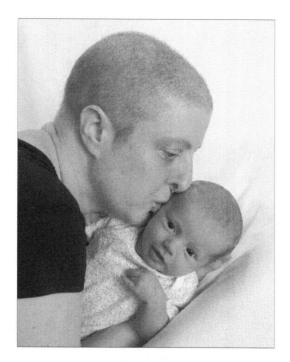

CHAPTER THIRTEEN: ALLISON

- Diagnosed 18 January 2013
- Invasive ductal carcinoma HER 2+, stage 1, grade 3
- Treatments during pregnancy: 6 Adriamycin/Cytoxan, 1 Taxol
- Delivered 21 May 2013
- Post-delivery treatments: 10 Taxol-low dose weekly, Herceptin

For God has not given us a spirit of fear and timidity,
but of power, love, and self-discipline.

2 Timothy 1:7

Survivorship: Living in the Aftermath

Chemotherapy, surgery, and cancer treatment is tough. It is strenuous physically, mentally, and emotionally. But I don't think I ever realized how difficult the recovery stage would be. In my opinion, and from my communication with many other cancer champions, I would say that "recovering" from the breast cancer experience is the toughest part.

In order to share this, I have to relive some difficult times, and it is not easy to be raw and exposed. But there were many times that I wished someone had warned me ahead of time about what I would experience. So I share this for those of you starting or travelling alongside someone in the journey. And to the doctors and medical staff out there: Always give us too much information. It may be hard to hear, but it is better to steel yourself going in than it is to suddenly hit an unexpected wall.

During Treatment

I was pregnant with my fifth child when I was diagnosed with breast cancer in January 2013. My oldest was ten years, my youngest was twenty-three months. I worked thirty hours per week as the Director of Elementary Education at our church and was doing my best to "keep up" with our active sons and daughters. I was forty-three years old, and my first trimester had been miserable with nausea, vomiting and fatigue. I was nineteen weeks pregnant when the doctor's office called me with the unexpected results from the needle biopsies of my breast tissue.

The diagnosis hit like a tornado. My life suddenly shifted to doctor appointments, a medical school crash course in Cancer 101, and life-altering decisions. Everything was sucked in and there was no time to think, only to react. I was fortunate to work in a church organization where everyone was completely supportive of me taking time off from work during my treatment. I trusted that people could fill in for me at work, but I knew I couldn't find a replacement wife/mom at home and I didn't think I could do both well.

My life consisted of two states of being. I was either at home with a toddler (and sometimes three other children) or at medical appointments and treatments (honestly, this was like a part-time job). The laundry didn't slow down. Family members still wanted to eat. Toys and dirt still wandered around the house. Hair and teeth needed brushing … and then four months later the world shifted *again*. We had a newborn. It was exhausting, but I was blessed with lots of help during this period in many ways. Meals, groceries, lunch box donations, babysitters, laundry folders, gift cards, cleaning, funds, cards, and prayers. And my mom, who had fought the cancer monster only a few years before.

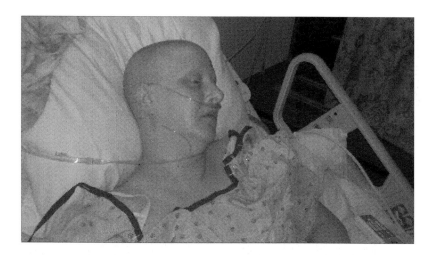

In the midst of this at one of my early chemotherapy appointments, the nurse talked to me about "survivorship." She explained that the cancer journey was tough and the oncology community had learned that they needed to help people beyond just the physical treatment to be "well" again. I took a ten-minute test on a little computer and passed with flying colors. I was coping very well, had lots of

support, a strong marriage, and was getting through the battle mentally healthy.

There is Joy

Every milestone in the cancer journey feels like a success to celebrate. *I finished my first chemo treatment. I shaved my hair. My baby is alive and well! My scan was clear! Last chemo. My mastectomy is done. My hair is growing back …*

Many of my cancer sisters are truly grateful through this experience. When you learn you have cancer when you are pregnant, your fight is not just for yourself, but with the fierce love of a mother for her child. Because of this, cancer moms are appreciative—ecstatically relieved even—to be alive to meet their beautiful newborn children. My daughter was my constant companion in my treatment and gave me extra motivation to persevere. In cancer treatment, the abnormal becomes normal. I remember a day when my oldest daughter and I went out somewhere and ended up eating ice cream cones while sitting in the sunshine on a sidewalk. I still remember that ordinary moment as a beautiful gift. Cancer makes you appreciate little things like ice cream or the presence of family and a supportive husband.

Life in the treatment phase exists in short bubbles of time, mostly to get through them and partly due to medication cycles. Every three weeks I had chemo. There was a pattern to this with how I felt, medical appointments, and the routine. Within each day, I took things as I could handle them, in short time periods. First, pack lunches and get the kids off to school. Take medication. Next, change the baby's diaper and feed the toddler breakfast. Feed myself. Sit and rest for twenty minutes. Empty dishwasher …

Because of this compartmentalized lifestyle, it was hard to fully deal with everything as it happened. I was hit with one loss after another without time to grieve each one. Then, suddenly, treatment was finished. I came out a "survivor" on the other side, with a cute little crew cut and did a double-take. "What just happened?!" I see this same cycle repeat itself with many of my cancer sisters.

My Hair Grew Back

Suddenly hair, eyebrows, and eyelashes come back, and you are no longer a "marked" cancer patient. With the normal appearance and end of chemo treatment, people believe that life is returning to "normal." On January 31, 2014, one year after my diagnosis and four months after my grueling double mastectomy and reconstruction surgery I wrote:

So, the adventure continues. These days I feel like the battle is largely mental. Do I focus on the *can* or *can't*? Do my pains and losses command my attention, or my hopes and thankfulness? Do I get mired in my frustrations or work past them? Am I short-tempered or cheerful? And I share this next thought as a point of insight, not for some expected action from my readers ... but I have learned that the cancer experience is much like that of someone who has lost a loved one. There is a great and immediate rallying of friends, family, neighbors, and strangers around the individual and family to support them through the crisis time in a variety of ways. But after the funeral (or after the treatment ends) and things appear to be normal again, the web of undergirding support is gone. So not only do you grieve the loss of the loved one, but the other burdens of daily life come back, too: cleaning, laundry, making a meal, paying bills, groceries, etc. I am not sure of a better way to explain it except that it is almost a double-hit back into the harsh world of reality. I am not through this yet, but now I am alone.

And so I walk into these days like a hike through a thick forest. Some parts of the trail are dark and overcast, while in another section beams of light streak between the leaves, and in some places the trail opens into a wide sunny patch where the light is warm, the sky is blue and filled with hope and peace....

It feels a lot like walking on a balance beam between giddy gratitude for being alive and a dark shadow that hovers nearby. But why?

Physical Changes

Let's start with the obvious. In the case of breast cancer, many of us have breast surgery. Obviously, this is a very personal space with a lot of emotional connections. There is the sexual aspect, the link to our femininity and appearance, and what I would describe as maternal connections.

From a physical standpoint, the artificial can never replace the natural. Never *ever* tell a woman who needs or has had breast surgery that at least she got a "boob job" out of it. Even as a joke. We have breast surgery because we believe it is necessary to save our lives, not because we want a larger or perkier chest. *It is not an elective surgery in our minds.* I remember one friend saying we feel like we have a gun pointed at our head and this is what we have to do to live.

Procedurally, the surgeries are also *very* different. In breast enhancement surgery, the natural breast tissue and nipples are not removed. In a mastectomy, most often the entire nipple is removed and much of the skin. The breast tissue beneath, which extends up to your collar bone, is removed. One or more lymph nodes under the armpit are also removed. After a mastectomy, there is little to no feeling left in the breasts. I can't speak for those who have had surgery for other types of cancer, but breast cancer attacks a very personal part of the feminine body. I am reminded of this often, and I feel a flicker of grief every time.

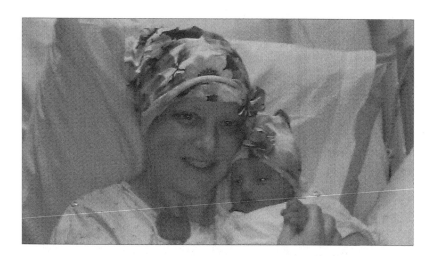

Many women have other physical changes as well. Achiness in joints or numbness in toes or fingers. A loss of menstruation and fertility. Scars from surgeries. Less hair than they used to have. A variety of things. In my case, the largest physical change I experienced is permanent damage to my heart muscle as a result of one my cancer drugs. I am able to function normally, but will be on heart medications for the rest of my life. On a minor note, my Brooke Shield-ish eyebrows have never grown back as full as they were. Whenever I put on makeup I am reminded of this loss in the mirror. Every person is different and the physical changes may be small or significant but regardless they serve as post-cancer reminders of losses.

Sexual and Relationship Challenges

In my opinion, a huge failing in modern cancer treatment is the lack of planned mental health care. At certain points in the journey, there should be set appointment checks with an experienced counselor. There is still too much stigma attached to mental health, or maybe a stubborn sense of self-reliance, but I have seen many of us get into a deep hole before seeking help on several levels.

Within every cancer support circle I was a part of, women expressed difficulties in their relationships with their husbands. I asked my plastic surgeon prior to surgery if most couples got through the process okay and recovered from all the changes. He said that his experience was that couples who had a strong relationship to begin with weathered the storm just fine and came out stronger. Those who had problems at the start had trouble staying together through the process.

Indeed, in the women I have known, there have been many stories of men who "couldn't take it" and left them and often, their children, in spite of the crisis of cancer. For those of us with devoted, patient partners we appreciate their sacrifice and love.

Starting with breast cancer diagnosis, there is a shift in how both partners feel about the breasts. For some women, the breast becomes the enemy, and they are eager to have it gone, almost in fear until it is removed. The breasts can also become "unappealing" to one or both partners. I have heard of men who were afraid to hurt their wives if they touched their breasts. On the other hand, women felt unloved when husbands no longer wanted to be intimate.

The cancer patient is most often bald. Post-surgery, there are scars and the breast area is just, well, *ugly*. For those of us who are also pregnant during cancer, we feel fat and freakish! I used to joke that I had two melons, my bald head and my big belly. As you might imagine, this is not conducive to romance! Add to this fact that the cancer drugs put us into a chemical menopause and suppress hormones, causing vaginal dryness. Women in cancer treatment are fatigued, can be less than enthusiastic about sex, hormonally speaking, and can experience pain during intercourse.

Over time, things do improve from an intimacy standpoint. Discomfort improves and couples learn to adjust to physical changes. From start to finish, my breast surgeries took nine months. In that time, I also had physical therapy for cording (Your arm feels like there is a puppet string inside, and you can't lift your arm all the way up). My chest pain is ninety-five percent gone. But in my case, the payment for having a chest that "looks good" is two silicone inserts behind my pectoral muscles. This does not feel natural, and I still have twinges of muscle pain. There are certain movements that make the chest look strange or unnatural. Again, this is not a boob job. My plastic surgeon remains one of my favorite doctors in this process and did excellent work. I am happy with the results of my surgery but on my worst days, I fear that sex will never be as enjoyable as it used to be. This doesn't diminish my love for my husband, but it is a somber thought.

Chemo Brain, Depression, PTSD

The most difficult adjustment in daily life is chemo brain (aka chemo fog, cognitive impairment, or cognitive dysfunction). An estimated twenty to thirty percent of cancer patients experience some long-term cognitive effects from chemotherapy.

Words to describe how this feels are ditzy, forgetful, lost, overwhelmed, stupid. Things like forgetting a word or a person's name, or forgetting to do something. While it may seem comical sometimes, it is frustrating and affects your quality of life and work.

One day, three of my kids were sitting on the couch. One complained of a headache, so I went to get her a pain tablet. I was talking to my husband while getting the tablet and water from the adjoining kitchen. I went back to the couch and gave the cup and pill to the child sitting in the middle of the couch. A minute later, I realized the intended child was not sitting there, but had stepped out of the room, and I had given the medication to the toddler instead! I took it away from him as he tried to chew on it, puzzled. My husband and I just shook our heads and took it in stride. Later that evening, I realized that after all of that I forgot to give the correct kid her pain pill at all!

This is one example. Fortunately not dangerous, but it could have been. My poor husband became used to me forgetting things but has to deal with the frustration of my errors constantly. "Did you put the laundry in the dryer?" No. "Did you deposit the checks at the bank?" No. "Did you make her practice her piano?" No. "Did you pick up milk at the store for breakfast?" No. "Did you ask the doctor about that?" No. Not only was he being Super-Hubby and -Dad to five, but he was picking up the slack from everything my brain couldn't keep up with.

I don't know whether I had it harder because I had four kids and a newborn or if it is this hard for everyone, but I felt overwhelmed. When things went smoothly, I could cope. But as soon as kids started fighting, or a glass of milk spilled on the floor, I was done. I was immobilized. It felt like I was in a haze, and I could only see what was immediately in front of me. On my toughest days, I concentrated on getting through hour by hour. I couldn't take more than one thing at a time, it felt like bullets hammering me whenever I had to multitask.

At some point, my husband remarked, "You seem like you should be normal by now." He didn't mean it in a cruel way, but just that he was surprised that after all this time, I was still struggling so much.

I remember going back to work part time and returning to more regular routines. People would ask me how I was doing, and I never knew if they wanted the long, honest answer or just the polite "fine." I had survived a health crisis and should be—and was—grateful to be alive. Did I really need to continue to "whine" about being tired, having pain, or constipation or memory loss or whatever? The irony was that while I had fought hard and was thankful to be alive, there were days when I definitely felt it would be easier not to be.

I finally sought help from a psychologist who worked regularly with cancer patients. After several months of meeting with her, I was ready to try some medication to help with the continued difficulties I was having. She helped me to understand that they were not a weakness or failure on my part, but that the cancer treatment had taken a toll not only on my body but also on my brain.

I found a short story my nine-year-old son wrote during the time I was in treatment. It was about a shark family:

> In the sea there was a friendly shark named Daffy, and he liked to be helpful. His dad was mean and grumpy and was always yelling at people. His mom always stayed up too late and was crabby.

I was reluctant to label what I was going through as depression, and I felt like I should be able to manage it with faith and perseverance. But my fatigue, short-temper, and feeling overwhelmed were all evidence of depression.

The medication, first Zoloft and later Prozac, made a huge difference for me. I didn't sink into despair and exhaustion so easily. I could see multiple things happening, and deal with them one at a time. ("First, get her glass of juice. Second, butter his toast. Third, sign the permission slip ...") I wasn't overwhelmed anymore, and I wanted others to know how to lift the cloud that follows after treatment.

Early in my diagnosis, I was fortunate to find another mom who had been in cancer treatment while pregnant on an online baby site. She invited me to join a Facebook group of moms who were pregnant with cancer called "Kick-Ass Cancer Mamas." This group became a lifeline. While I have never met most of these women face-to-face, they have become like sisters to me. We take turns complaining, encouraging, venting, seeking advice, celebrating, and grieving together.

Many women face a fear of recurrence. With every weird body symptom or routine scan, the brain jumps to "What if the cancer is back?" Some have gone back to treatment after a recurrence and successfully conquered the disease. Other ladies in this group have lost their lives to cancer, and this is devastating to those "left behind." It feels so cruel that some of us are blessed to continue on while other friends are unfairly and randomly taken from this life.

How do you embrace healing and life and move ahead, while keeping one foot in the door of the cancer club? At one point, I felt like I needed to just step away from Facebook to be a part of the new reality of my daily life. It was hard to be present in that place where there was so much pain and so many hard memories. And to give my family and "life" the attention it deserved.

Many people who go through cancer treatment experience PTSD (post-traumatic stress disorder).* And I understand this now. Like soldiers in a battleground, women who have fought cancer have come through a very different and harsh reality. Like a wounded veteran with an artificial leg, we look normal on the outside, but our prosthetic body parts are not the same as the originals. We have made sacrifices to be alive and are thankful to be here. But our hearts are still with our comrades in the battle and we have guilt leaving them fighting in the trenches without us. We strive to live fully with the "second chance" we are given, but there are occasions when you feel you have to look behind and make sure the cancer beast is not following you.

There is a balance that must be found. I realized that God brought me through my journey, and I needed to share it and use it to support others. I returned to the Facebook group and have tried to be a voice of encouragement to my sisters there. I draw strength and inspiration from these beautiful souls who understand this journey better than anyone else.

We remember the friends we have lost together. We seek advice and solace. We admire our beautiful "chemo babies" and give hope to the newcomers. To date, there are 161 members in this group of women. Some of those members are no longer on this planet, but we occasionally see photos of the families they left behind and their growing children. A sign of the legacy they leave behind.

Getting Through

One of the biggest blessings in the cancer journey for me was the people. I would be remiss if I did not explain how a village of people helped me through this process.

First, I would tell you to advocate for yourself health-wise. Follow your gut, and do not be afraid to get a second opinion—or third!—until you find a doctor who listens and whom you have a good rapport with. It is critical to trust the team who is trying to save the life of you and your baby! My husband and I didn't have a good feeling after meeting with the first oncologist we saw. Two days later and in another office across town, we met a second oncologist who inspired confidence and hope, and we knew he was the clear choice. All along my path, there are clearly medical professionals who I credit with their part in my recovery. Our obstetrician, perinatologists, oncology experts, general surgeons, my cardiologist, my plastic surgeon, physical therapists, psychologists, my general practitioner, and several really special nurses. When one doctor doesn't work out, don't give up. Keep trying and asking until you find who you need.

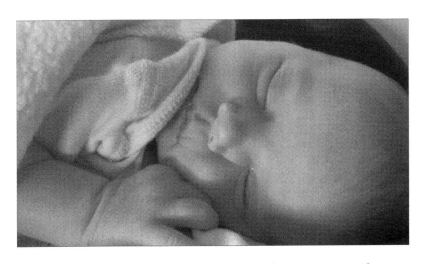

People came from unexpected places to assist us. A mom from my daughter's class whom I didn't even know called and asked to come to the house and do whatever I needed. She was one of my most hands-on helpers and became a friend. Others were relatives or came from church or the neighborhood. It is a surprising experience to see who comes to your aid when you are ill. Those who you might expect to help are often not the ones who make the biggest impact.

And other cancer warriors are the ones whose shoulders you can cry on. You can ask them gross questions, complain about rude comments you've heard, compare medical treatment, and share photos of your beautiful kids. The support of others who understand the challenging stages of this process are critical and it helps you feel a little less crazy and lonely.

And God was and is my Rock. To those whom this seems like a cliché, I apologize. But until you have relied on your faith and conversations with an unseen person and found Him never to be lacking, I suppose it is hard to understand. No human can possibly support someone entirely through this cancer experience. No one is that strong or has all the answers. But God *never* let me down, always met me where I was—high or low—and gave me the words, the grace, the joke, or song I needed to hear. It is to Him that I continue to go and to entrust my future.

I still grieve the things I have lost from cancer. I know I will never be the same. But I stroke the face of my daughter or watch my children laugh and give praise for being alive. The bottom line is that every day is a gift, whether it is a good day or a hard day. I have learned to make peace with whatever comes. I accept the gifts and endure the pain.

* *"The incidence of the full syndrome of PTSD (meeting full DSM-IV diagnostic criteria) ranges from 3% to 4% in early-stage patients recently diagnosed to 35% in patients evaluated after treatment. When incidence of PTSD-like symptoms (not meeting the full diagnostic criteria) is measured, the rates are higher, ranging from 20% in patients with early-stage cancer to 80% in those with recurrent cancer." National Cancer Institute, January 2015*

Acknowledgments

A glimpse into a life, just a moment, a piece of a great thousand-piece puzzle. That's what these chapters are. Each of these women have chosen a part of their battle with cancer to share, working together harmoniously to see cancer and pregnancy as it is from different perspectives and experiences.

Allison Graefe Burkhow Blessed with a loving, crazy family, including five kids and husband, Jon. Kept afloat by faith in God. Children's Ministry worker and movie lover.

Heather Choate A #1 bestselling author, marriage coach, and mother of six amazing, rowdy children. She credits her survival of cancer while pregnant to God and her unconditionally-loving husband, Ben. Visit her at www.heatherchoate.com

Robin Cox Cordry Born 27 October 1964, became a mother 29 November 1999, became a survivor on 22 March 2005, and my miracle chemo baby arrived 6 November 2005. Every day since than has been infused with a will to thrive.

Tiffany Davis A three-year survivor of choriocarcinoma and battles multiple sclerosis. She spends her days drinking coffee, teaching fifth grade, and raising her two greatest blessings, Brian and Aubrey. She loves going to movies with her husband, Tom, and adventuring away from her small town in Ohio, especially on road trips.

Diana Fodor Mother, daughter, sister, wife, friend, lover of any corny shark movie, slowly learning to dance in the rain again.

Dee Hinote Mother to her one and only sweet potato, Benjamin. Married to her lifelong travel companion and best friend, Jeremy. Particularly fond of Disney World, dogs, and iced coffee.

Amy Lacoste Defined by a New Englander's heart and a Californian's soul, Amy spends her workdays lost in translation and her weekends immersed in bargain-hunting, gardening, and caring for friends and family, both two-legged and four. She still hasn't decided what she wants to be when she grows up.

Stephanie Partridge Stephanie strives to follow her Lord and God each day. He is the source of her joy and gratitude. She daydreams of the Puget Sound and lives in the desert. She admires her husband and loves her five boys.

Lauren Hubert Smoke Lover of life, guitar, songwriting, teaching music, children, and yoga. Blessed mother of Nico, her hero and everything. Loved by Ian, her companion and friend. Fierce.

Jennifer Stewart A loving mom to two amazing kiddos and a two-time cancer survivor, Jenn loves teaching, being out in nature, cooking great food, and spending time with her family and close friends.

Caitlin Sticka Believer in God and His faithfulness, wife to her best friend, mama to two beautiful daughters. Teacher. Lover of thrift shopping and binge-watching HGTV and The Ellen Show.

Heather Trieu A mother of two of her own and also two step-children, Heather lives in Minnesota with her husband and two girls and works as a school counselor.

Barbara Vlachos Adventure-seeker, outdoorswoman, lover of life, former vagabond returned home. Married her dream man she knew as a child.

Mother of two wild and wonderful little boys. Faithful servant sharing the light.

Made in the USA
Lexington, KY
10 July 2017